INVERCLYDE LIBRARIES

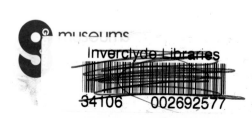

museums
Inverclyde Libraries

34106   002692577

Opposite: Glen Moss, Kilmacolm © T Norman Tait.

First published in 2010 by Culture and Sport Glasgow (Glasgow Museums).

Text © Culture and Sport Glasgow (Glasgow Museums) 2010.
Design and typography © Culture and Sport Glasgow (Glasgow Museums) 2010.
All images © Culture and Sport Glasgow (Glasgow Museums) 2010 unless otherwise acknowledged.

ISBN 978-0-902752-96-2

The format of this book was inspired by *Archaeology Around Glasgow: 50 remarkable sites to visit* by Susan Hothersall, first published in 2007 by Culture and Sport Glasgow (Glasgow Museums).

Authors

Introduction: Alastair Gunning, Richard Sutcliffe, Keith Watson and Olivia Lassiere.
Site descriptions as numbered in the book: 1 Sheila Russell, 2 and 3 Jim Coyle, 4 Alastair Gunning, 5 Sven Rasmussen and Ross MacLeod, 6 Paul Matthews, 7 Jenny Tweedie and Cath Scott, 8 Jimmy Huis and Carol Maclean, 9 Sandy McNeil, 10 Dave Garner, 11 Ian Boyd, 12 Richard Bolton and Eilidh Milne, 13 Richard Sutcliffe and Gary Linstead, 14 Keith Watson, 15 Alastair Gunning, 16 Gillian Neil and Gillian Telfer, 17 Susan Futter and Gillian Telfer, 18 Alastair Gunning, 19 Tim Jacobs, 20 Richard Sutcliffe and Alastair Gunning, 21 East Dunbartonshire and Mugdock Country Park Ranger Service, 22 Richard Sutcliffe, 23 Dave Garner, 24 David Shenton, 25 Alastair Gunning, 26 Neil DL Clark, 27 Jeanne Robinson, 28 David Pickett, 29 and 30 East Dunbartonshire and Mugdock Country Park Ranger Service, 31 Duncan Clark, 32 Richard Sutcliffe, 33–36 Clyde Muirshiel Regional Park and Iain P Gibson, 37 Paula Baker, 38 Iain P Gibson, 39 T Norman Tait, 40 Iain P Gibson, 41 Petrina Brown, 42 Gill Smart, 43 Richard Sutcliffe, 44 Gill Smart, 45 Kim McEwen, 46–48 Louisa Hancock, 49 Toby Wilson, 50 Steve Blow.

Devised and co-ordinated by Richard Sutcliffe
Edited by Richard Sutcliffe and Kim Teo
Designed by John Westwell
Glasgow Museums' photography by Ellen Howden and Jim Dunn, with additional images by Alastair Gunning, Jeanne Robinson, Richard Sutcliffe, Keith Watson.

Printed in Scotland by Allander.

Supported by the Glasgow Natural History Society.

www.glasgowmuseums.com

Wildlife Around Glasgow

50 remarkable sites to explore

Contents

Foreword

I am lucky to have been working in the field of wildlife and nature conservation in Glasgow for the past 21 years and am proud to have been elected as the first chairman of a group of organizations – now the Glasgow Biodiversity Partnership – that have agreed to work together to preserve, improve and create habitats in the city.

However, long before my professional involvement, I first became interested in wildlife when still at primary school, as a result of my parents moving from a modern tenement to a prefab on the edge of Maryhill in north Glasgow. The house lay adjacent to a field used for grazing horses and we had outstanding views of farmland and, in the distance, the Campsie Fells. I was amazed at the different birds, butterflies and mammals that visited our garden, with the highlights being redstart and grey partridge! I was encouraged by my primary-school teacher and I can still remember being taken on trips to Possil Marsh and making regular visits to Dawsholm Park and out into the countryside along the River Kelvin.

Some 45 years later, the views of the countryside from where our prefab used to be have been replaced by the Summerston housing estate. However, the site of the house and the adjoining field is now a Site of Local Importance for Nature Conservation; Possil Marsh is a Scottish Wildlife Trust Reserve; the flood plain of the River Kelvin at Millichen is a Site of City-wide Importance for Nature Conservation; and Dawsholm Park has been declared as a Local Nature Reserve by Glasgow City Council.

So, whilst much land has been taken for development, it is good to be able to acknowledge that many of the places that I went to as a young boy can still be visited today. In addition, as can be seen from the publication of this book, there are many other greenspaces to be enjoyed.

I would urge all of you to explore the sites described in this book – there are many surprises to be found and, I am sure, some discoveries about nature still to be made.

Jim Coyle MBE

The north-east entrance to Dawsholm Park.

© Richard Sutcliffe

Acknowledgements

This book is the result of the work of more than 40 individual authors, many representing diverse organizations related to natural history: Jim Coyle MBE; Susan Futter; T Norman Tait; Olivia Lassiere (British Waterways Scotland); Clyde Muirshiel Regional Park staff; Richard Bolton, Eilidh Milne (Dams to Darnley Country Park); East Dunbartonshire and Mugdock Country Park Ranger Service; Gillian Telfer (East Dunbartonshire Council); Ian Boyd, Dave Garner, Jimmy Huis, Gary Lindstead, Carol Maclean, Sandy McNeil, Paul Matthews, Sheila Russell, Cath Scott (Glasgow City Council); Alastair Gunning, Jeanne Robinson, Richard Sutcliffe, Keith Watson (Glasgow Museums); Dr Neil DL Clark (Hunterian Museum, University of Glasgow); Petrina Brown (Inverclyde, East Renfrewshire and Renfrewshire LBAP Partnership); Jackie Gilliland (North Lanarkshire Council); Paula Baker, Jenny Tweedie, Toby Wilson (RSPB); Tim Jacobs, David Pickett (Scottish Natural Heritage); Iain P Gibson (Scottish Ornithologists' Club); Steve Blow, Duncan Clark, Kim McEwen, Sven Rasmussen, David Shenton, Gill Smart (Scottish Wildlife Trust); Louisa Hancock (South Lanarkshire Council Countryside and Greenspace Service); Ross MacLeod (University of Glasgow); Gillian Neil (West Dunbartonshire Council).

I would like to thank all my co-authors for their contributions and for submitting, checking and rechecking text and images in order to meet ever-nearer deadlines.

Several other people provided useful information or checked drafts of the text, for which I am very grateful, in particular: John Pressley and Nicola McIntyre (Paisley Museum), Steve Edwards (Renfrewshire Council), Dr JW Faithfull and Geoff Hancock (Hunterian Museum, University of Glasgow), Michael Pink (Hamilton NHS), Geof Flann, Allison Greig (Glasgow City Council) and Joanna Harrison (British Waterways, Scotland).

I am also grateful to the many authors and the following people who have provided or made available photographs for the book: Dr Colin Bean, Bryan Bowes, Tom Byars, Ewan Douglas, Jim Duncan, Chris Everett, Gavin Finbow, Ian Fulton, Keith Futter, John Hawell, Bill Higgins, Bob Lambie, Robert McLeod, Malcolm Muir, David Palmar, Christine Sutcliffe, Jody Warner, Richard Weddle, Atom Photographic Agency, Glasgow City Council, Glasgow Natural History Society, the Hunterian Museum (University of Glasgow), the Natural History Museum, North Lanarkshire Council, RSPB Images, the Science Photo Library and South Lanarkshire Council Countryside Ranger Service. I must especially thank Norman Tait for his superb images – especially for the one of greylag geese on the cover – and also David Palmar, who came up trumps to fill some gaps at the last minute.

Special thanks are due to the Glasgow Natural History Society (Blodwyn Lloyd Binns Bequest) for generous financial support towards the production of this book.

And finally, a huge thank you to colleagues Alastair Gunning and Keith Watson for their significant contributions and Kim Teo and John Westwell, who edited and designed the book, without whom it would not be such a great success.

Richard Sutcliffe

How to use this book

Locating the sites

The map opposite shows the locations of the 50 main sites featured in this book, which are grouped by area. A more detailed map can be found at the start of each chapter.

In addition to the sketch maps and directions provided, each of the 50 site descriptions includes at least one six-figure Ordnance Survey grid reference so you can locate the site on Ordnance Survey maps – from either the Landranger (1:50,000 scale) or Explorer (1:25,000 scale) series.

For details of how to use a grid reference, see under 'Technical Information' on Landranger maps and 'The National Grid Reference System' on Explorer maps. Although officially written without, we have added spaces to the grid references in this book for ease of reading.

For more urban sites, a local street map will be useful. For sites of a particular geological interest, the relevant Geological Survey maps are listed.

Getting to the sites

Unless otherwise stated, all directions given are from the centre of Glasgow. We have included details of public transport where applicable. However, as services and timetables are subject to change, it is advisable to check when planning your journey. Strathclyde Partnership for Travel (SPT) has travel centres at Buchanan Bus Station and St Enoch Square, or you can phone 0141 332 6811, or look on their website www.spt.co.uk. Information about transport is also available from Travel Line Scotland (tel. 0871 200 2233, www.travelinescotland.com) and on the website www.firstgroup.com. For a few of the sites, if travelling by public transport it may ease the journey to arrange for a taxi to take you on the final leg.

Access to the sites and facilities

The sites are open at all times unless specified otherwise. Wheelchair access is noted where available. Facilities such as toilets and visitor centres are also detailed if present. Note that some visitor centres may be closed on public holidays.

Sites on private land

Please be aware that some of the sites are on privately owned land. Visitors have a responsibility to ensure that they cause no damage or disturbance. Please respect conditions imposed by landowners, remember to close gates and keep dogs under control.

Care for sites and yourself

Parts of some of the sites in this book are sensitive to disturbance. Please keep to paths where possible and abide by any signs relating to restricted access: ground-nesting birds and delicate plants could be damaged otherwise. Some species are legally protected and should not be disturbed at any time.

The terrain of the sites in this book varies. Sensible footwear is recommended and in some cases it may be a good idea to take waterproofs, food and drink, a first aid kit and insect repellent.

Enjoy Scotland's outdoors – responsibly!

Everyone has the right to be on most land and inland waterways providing they act responsibly. Your access rights and responsibilities are explained fully in the Scottish Outdoor Access Code, available at www.outdooraccess-scotland.com. The key things are to take responsibility for your own actions, respect the interests of other people and care for the environment.

If you intend to collect any fossils, you should be aware of the Scottish Fossil Code, which is available at www.snh.org.uk/fossilcode.

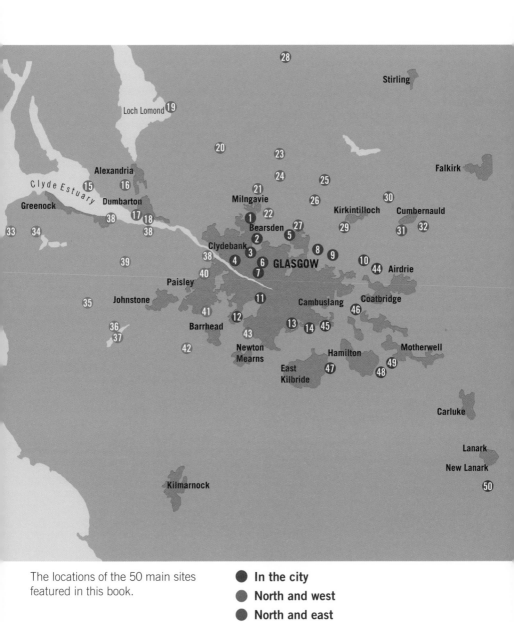

The locations of the 50 main sites featured in this book.

- ● In the city
- ● North and west
- ● North and east
- ● West
- ● South and east

Introduction: Natural history in and around Glasgow

Greater Glasgow has a human population of about 1.2 million people. Despite its industrial past, Scotland's largest city is also home to a surprising amount and variety of wildlife. About one fifth of the total area of the city is greenspace. This includes many old private estates that have been surrounded by urban developments, but which have retained a rich biodiversity. The city is crossed by several rivers, the Forth & Clyde Canal and railways, which all form wildlife corridors. Even motorways, often bounded by wide verges, trees and shrubs, are important. There are many

Wildlife is all around us: feral pigeons in George Square, Glasgow.

© Christine Sutcliffe

designated wildlife sites in the area, including Local Nature Reserves, Sites of Special Scientific Interest and Sites of Importance for Nature Conservation.

In the north-east of Glasgow the Bishop's Estate extends into North Lanarkshire and connects, by way of Johnston Loch, to Drumpellier Country Park, making it one of the largest lowland wetland complexes in central Scotland. Just to the north of the city is Mugdock Country Park, with its ancient woodland, and further north is Flanders Moss, one of the most intact lowland raised bogs in the UK, and the Loch Lomond and the Trossachs National Park.

To the south-east are Calderglen and Chatelherault country parks, and the Clyde Valley woodlands leading to the Falls of Clyde. To the west of Glasgow the River Clyde widens into the Clyde Estuary, an area of great importance for many birds and of international importance for its population of redshanks. In Renfrewshire there is Gleniffer Braes Country Park, and in Inverclyde Clyde Muirshiel Regional Park, an area mainly of high moorland and the largest regional park in Scotland.

These diverse and wonderful places and all the other sites described in this book have been happy hunting grounds for naturalists for more than 160 years and still continue to be so today.

Opposite: Small totoiseshell butterfly beside the M8 motorway in Glasgow.

© Cath Scott

Geology

The geology of the area covered by this book is amazingly varied in terms of both age and rock type. This diversity is the product of Scotland's journey through geological time: over hundreds of millions of years Scotland, and the tectonic plate it is a part of, has drifted across the globe and been subject to different climates and changing environments, from ocean floor to baking desert. This brief overview will highlight some of the more important features and stories told by the rocks.

The bedrock or solid rock geology ranges in age from the Dalradian to the early Permian, reflecting a time span in the order of 440 million years. Much of the bedrock dates from the Carboniferous Period; Silurian and Devonian age rocks are also present.

The bedrock is mostly covered by much younger superficial deposits. These unconsolidated sediments include till (also known as boulder clay) and sands and gravels deposited by glaciers and

Simplified map of the geology of the Glasgow area.

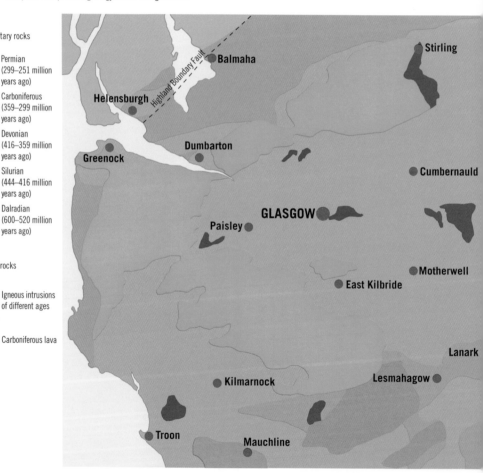

Sedimentary rocks

Permian
(299–251 million
years ago)

Carboniferous
(359–299 million
years ago)

Devonian
(416–359 million
years ago)

Silurian
(444–416 million
years ago)

Dalradian
(600–520 million
years ago)

Igneous rocks

Igneous intrusions
of different ages

Carboniferous lava

Stirling

Balmaha

Highland Boundary Fault

Helensburgh

Dumbarton

Greenock

Cumbernauld

GLASGOW

Paisley

Motherwell

East Kilbride

Lanark

Kilmarnock

Lesmahagow

Troon

Mauchline

meltwaters during the Ice Age, sediments associated with changes in sea level, recent river deposits and peat.

Dalradian *600–520 million years ago*
The Highland Boundary fault, a major fracture in the Earth's crust, runs through the area covered by this book, across the southern end of Loch Lomond. The change of scenery across the Highland line reflects a major difference in the rocks on either side. Immediately to the south there are softer sedimentary rocks. To the north there are hard metamorphic rocks of the

Highlands known as the Dalradian.

Dalradian rocks are ancient and have a complex history. They were originally deposited as sediments in an ocean, known as the Iapetus, on the edge of a continent, Laurentia. A 25km-thick pile of sediments built up. These consolidated to form layers of rock – sandstone, mudstone and greywacke. Then, as a result of plate tectonic movements in the Earth's crust, the Iapetus Ocean began to close. As another continent approached Laurentia,

Satellite image of the Glasgow area.

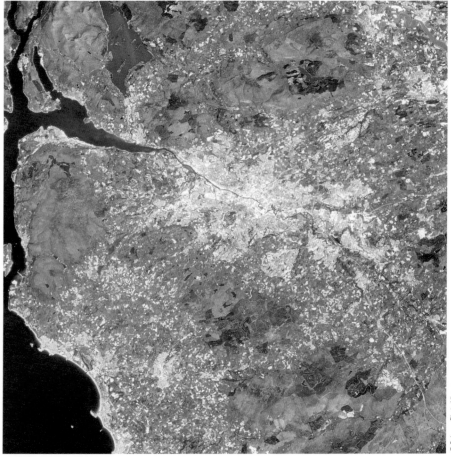

Graphite schist. (Glasgow Museums, no. DB.3166)

the intervening sedimentary rocks were squeezed by immense forces. In this environment, where they were subject to high temperatures and pressure, the rocks were metamorphosed, buckled and deformed into the schists, slates and phyllites we find today. In a process that occurred over many millions of years, they were forced up to form a mountain chain similar in scale to the Himalayas.

Conic Hill runs parallel to the line of the Highland Boundary Fault, which is just to the north.

© David C Shenton

Silurian *444–416 million years ago*
Before the Silurian Period, the rocks that were to form Scotland and England and Wales were on different continents separated by the Iapetus Ocean. They were brought together around 425 million years ago, when the Iapetus completely closed and the two continents collided.

Silurian rocks – conglomerates, sandstones, siltstone and mudstones – are to be found in the high ground west of Lesmahagow. For much of the time when the sediments that formed these rocks were laid down, the area was under water; the rocks mark the transition from marine to lagoons and deltas and then to terrestrial conditions. Some of the layers contain rare fossils and the Lesmahagow Silurian is famous for its internationally important fish and arthropod remains. The primitive jawless fish are amongst the oldest complete fish known. The rich fauna of arthropods includes eurypterids – water scorpions – such as *Slimonia* and *Erettopterus*, and the pod shrimp *Ceratiocaris*. The sites where these occur are protected and no specimens should be collected.

Fossil water scorpion *Erettopterus bilobus*. (Glasgow Museums, no. 1901.123.gq)

Devonian *416–359 million years ago*
There are rocks that date to the Devonian Period occupying the tract of lower ground running between the Highland Boundary Fault to the north and the Kilpatrick Hills and Campsie Fells to the south. There are also smaller outcrops on the Clyde coast south from Wemyss Bay and around Lanark. These rocks are mostly red sandstones and conglomerates, and for this reason these Devonian rocks are also known as the Old Red Sandstone.

Following the collision of the two continents containing Scotland and England and Wales during the preceding Silurian Period, Scotland was in the middle of a combined land mass. Its landscape consisted of mountain ranges with intervening lowland basins. Scotland was to the south of the equator and the climate was hot and arid. Desert conditions prevailed.

In general terms, what is now the Midland Valley was a basin between mountains and areas of higher ground. Large rivers and streams emanating from the early Highlands and Southern Uplands, and from mountainous areas further afield, flowed across this lowland. These rivers carried enormous amounts of sediment eroded from the upland areas. The Devonian sandstones and conglomerates seen today represent the sand, gravel, pebbles and boulders deposited by the rivers as they flowed into and across the basins. The coarser material was dropped first, while finer sand was washed further into the low ground. Thick layers of conglomerate occur just south of the Highland Boundary Fault and can be seen at Aberfoyle and Balmaha. At the latter, conglomerate forms the prominent ridge of Conic Hill. Devonian rocks can also be seen at Ardmore Point and the Falls of Clyde (see pp. 84 and 166).

Carboniferous *359–299 million years ago*
Rocks of Carboniferous age underlie Glasgow itself and a large part of the surrounding area. By Carboniferous times

Scotland had drifted close to the equator and was subject to a hot and humid climate. The deserts of the Devonian gave way to coastal plains and lagoons, often highly saline because of evaporation in the hot climate. The earliest Carboniferous rocks were deposited in this environment. These rocks include the Ballagan Formation – layers of shale and cementstone – named after Ballagan Glen (see p. 100), where they are well exposed. After this transition period the Carboniferous was a time of tropical forests, shallow coral seas and volcanoes.

Throughout much of the Carboniferous Period the environment was one of river plains and deltas. These extensive areas of low-lying, swampy land were swathed in lush tropical rainforests. The scene would have looked rather like the present-day Amazon, but with different trees and plants. The fossil remains of these plants – giant clubmosses, horsetails and ferns – are relatively common and can be found, for example, on old coal bings. Fossil Grove in Glasgow is an exceptional site where a small part of one of these forests is preserved (see p. 54).

Time after time throughout the Carboniferous this landscape was submerged by the sea. During the early Carboniferous the flooding created warm, shallow seas with coral reefs reminiscent of parts of the Caribbean Sea today. Marine life flourished in these waters. They were home to corals and sponges, to bivalve, gastropod and cephalopod molluscs, and to brachiopods, crinoids, trilobites and a variety of other life forms. Fossils of these animals have been found at many sites around Glasgow, including Blairskaith Quarry (see p. 108), Corrie Burn near Kilsyth (NS 683 782) and Trearne Quarry near Beith (NS 372 533). A wide variety of fish also swam in the Carboniferous sea, but their fossil

Fossil cone *Lepidostrobus sp.* (Glasgow Museums, no. G.1981.128)

Artist's impression of a Carboniferous forest, based on the remains preserved at Fossil Grove.

The Bearsden Shark, *Akmonistion zangerli*.
(Hunterian Museum, no. V8246)

remains are not so common. A rich fauna of beautifully preserved fish including sharks was found at Bearsden.

This cycle of change is recorded in the rocks layers. Throughout the Carboniferous rock sequence, rocks deposited as sediment on the sea floor alternate with terrestrial sediments, including sandstone laid down by rivers and coal formed from thick piles of forest plant debris.

The Carboniferous was not all tranquillity: volcanic activity was widespread. Around 340 million years ago volcanoes spewed out lava across the landscape of the Glasgow area. Over millions of years there were many eruptions, mainly of basalt lava. Individual flows built up into a pile nearly 1km thick at its maximum. These lavas, known as the Clyde Plateau Volcanic Formation, now form the high ground around Glasgow – the Campsie Fells and Kilpatrick Hills to the north and uplands including the the Renfrewshire hills and Eaglesham Moor south of the Clyde. The lavas were erupted through numerous volcanic vents – Dumbarton Rock (see p. 90), Dumgoyne (NS 541 827) and Duntreath (NS 531 810) near Strathblane are good examples.

Glasgow is built on Carboniferous rocks both literally and figuratively. The underlying coal seams helped fuel its growth into a large industrial city. Many of its tenements and other buildings use Carboniferous blond sandstone quarried within and around its confines. Carboniferous rocks have also provided other raw materials such as ironstone, limestone, fireclay and roadstone.

Permian *299–251 million years ago*
Rocks of Permian age occupy a small patch on the very southern limit of the Glasgow area. By the Permian, Scotland had continued on its journey north and was again subject to hot, arid conditions. In the desert environment wind-blown sand accumulated and created large dunes, which formed sandstone. About 260 million years old, these Permian rocks are mainly red sandstone and are sometimes called the New Red Sandstone (to differentiate them from the older red sandstones of the Devonian). The rock walls of the River Ayr gorge near Mauchline provide excellent exposures of the brick-red sandstone, within which the curved layering or dune bedding of the ancient sand dunes can be observed. At this locality the sandstones can be seen to overlie lava, also of Permian Age. Close by, Ballochmyle Quarry, now infilled, once supplied stone for some of Glasgow's red tenements.

Ice Age and after *The last 2.5 million years*
The Ice Age began around 2.5 million years ago. It was not a continuous glacial period: climate changes resulted in repeated advances and retreats of the ice sheets. Most of the glacial deposits around Glasgow relate to the more recent stages of the Ice Age – the last 30,000 years – as those of earlier times were swept away by later ice advances. From 30,000 to 15,000 years ago Scotland was in the grip of glacial conditions and was

Dunglass, a crag-and-tail feature.

blanketed by thick ice. This was followed by a warmer period – the Windermere Interstadial – which lasted until 12,900 years ago. Cold conditions then returned in a period known as the Loch Lomond Stadial, but the glaciers did not reach any further south than Drymen. The ice finally disappeared only 11,500 years ago.

Our present landscape owes much to the effects of the ice both through erosion and deposition. Corries on the north face of the Campsies, the largest of which is the Corrie of Balglass (NS 590 860), mark the head of former glaciers flowing off these hills. Crag-and-tail features, of which the Necropolis Hill in Glasgow (NS 605 655) and Dunglass near Strathblane (NS 575 789) are examples, are produced by ice moulding. Small rocky hills of hard and resistant igneous rock, the crags, were scoured by glaciers. The tails, sloping off one side of the hill and made up of softer sediment, were protected from erosion in the lee of the crag.

Throughout the Glasgow area much of the ground is blanketed by glacial deposits. Till is the rock debris carried by ice and then deposited on low ground. It consists of a mixture of clay with larger constituents ranging in size from gravel to pebbles and sometimes huge boulders. Till covers large areas around Glasgow. As the ice moved over the till it shaped it to form long, narrow steep-sided hills known as drumlins. The city is built on many drumlins, hence the large number of place names ending in 'hill'. Gilmorehill (NS 568 666) on which Glasgow University is built, nearby Park Circus (NS 574 663) and the hill in Bellahouston Park (NS 549 637) are all drumlins.

Other deposits, mainly sand and gravel, are associated with glacial meltwater streams and rivers that emanated from the glaciers. Thick deposits of these infill old buried channels of the Kelvin and

Drumlin, Bellahouston Park.

© Alastair Gunning

Clyde. Around Bishopbriggs and Cadder the near-surface sands and gravels of the Kelvin were extensively quarried. Sands and gravels associated with the glacier of the Loch Lomond Stadial occur to the east of Drymen.

The coming and going of the ice sheets resulted in changes in sea level. Old sea cliffs inland of the present coastline were formed when the sea level was higher than today. These, often obvious features, can be seen along much of the Clyde coast, including at Lunderston Bay (p. 126) and Ardmore Point (p. 84) and the Cardross area. The level ground between these cliffs and the present shoreline is often overlain by beach deposits and is known as a raised beach.

During the Windermere Interstadial, a time of ice retreat, the sea level was up to 40m higher than today. Marine water penetrated into the Glasgow area and Loch Lomond became an arm of the sea.

Raised beach and cliff at Portencross.

The marine clay deposited on the bed of this inland sea forms extensive areas of flat land on either side of the Clyde. It contains fossil shells including species that today are found much further north, indicating that colder conditions prevailed. After the end of the Ice Age, the sea level was also higher in relation to the land than it is today. But since then the land has risen – because of the removal of the weight of the ice sheets – and the present relationship between land and sea has become established.

Deposition has continued since the Ice Age. Sand and gravel alluvium borders the Clyde and its tributaries. Peat has accumulated both on upland areas, including the Campsie Fells and Kilpatrick Hills, and to form lowland raised bogs at Flanders Moss (see p. 114) and Linwood and Barochan Mosses to the north of Linwood.

Climate

The climate in and around Glasgow is strongly influenced by how far north the area is and the Atlantic to the west. It is characteristically an oceanic climate, with equable, mild temperatures, high amounts of rainfall and cloud cover, and frequent strong winds. This Atlantic climate is shared with other European countries, from western France, across the Low Countries and to western Scandinavia. Within central Glasgow, temperatures are slightly higher due to the urban heat island effect.

Weather data relevant to the area is available from the Meteorological Office's weather station at Paisley, and also from the Coats Observatory at Paisley Museum, where detailed records have been kept since 1885. These show a general trend of rising temperatures and increased rainfall, notably in the last ten years. This is in line with the consensus of measurements taken across the world.

Temperatures

Analysis of 125 years of data shows that average monthly temperatures are increasing, with, over the whole period, an increase of around 0.5 degree Celsius in the winter months, and around one degree in March, May, August and October. Much of the increase has occurred relatively recently.

The average monthly mean temperature over the last 30 years was recorded as 9.5 degrees, with the period 2000–2009 averaging 10.0 degrees. On the Ayrshire coast the average temperature is generally higher, while in the hills it is lower.

April to October are the seven months when the average temperature exceeds six degrees, commonly accepted as the threshold for plant growth, though frosts can occur in April and October, and occasionally in May.

Rainfall

The amount of rainfall in the area – along with hail, sleet and snow – is strongly influenced by location. There is generally more rain in the west than the east. Greenock receives over 1500mm of rain each year, whereas the highest ground of the West Renfrewshire Heights gets over 2400mm. By contrast, in the drier south-

Mean temperature chart based on data from the Coats Observatory at Paisley Museum.

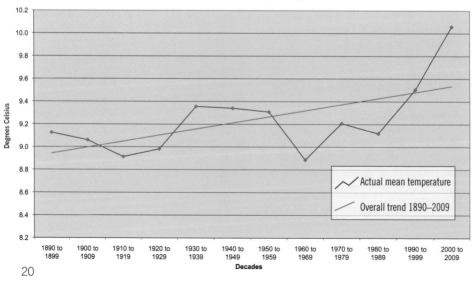

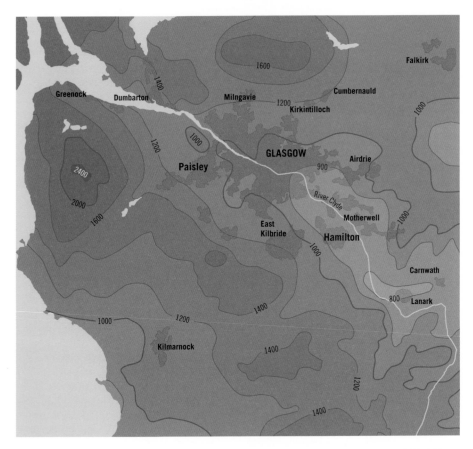

east, the Clyde Valley between Motherwell and Carnwath receives less than 900mm. The rainfall is marked not so much for its quantity or intensity but its frequency.

The records show that there has been a general trend over the last 125 years of the winters getting wetter and the summers dryer, and spring and autumn becoming slightly wetter. There is greatly increased rainfall from September to March, a slight increase in April to June, a slight decrease in July and a large decrease in August. The average yearly rainfall from 1980–2009 was 1249.3mm.

The combination of high rainfall and low or mild temperatures encourages the formation of waterlogged or poorly drained soil types and the formation of organic

Average annual rainfall (mm) for the period 1941–1970. Adapted from *The Climate of Great Britain Climatological Memorandum 124 Glasgow and the Clyde Valley*, published by the Meteorological Office, Edinburgh, 1981.

peats (for example, moorland and mires). This means that there is a low risk of drought conditions inhibiting plant growth in the wetter west and uplands, although there is a chance of this in the drier south-east.

Sunshine

The amount of sunshine received in the area has generally increased over the last 125 years. Winters are getting slightly sunnier, while springs and summers are getting duller except for peaks in May

21

Rainfall totals chart based on data from the Coats Observatory at Paisley Museum.

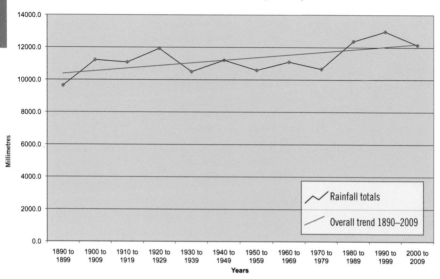

and August, and September remains unchanged. In common with many parts of western Scotland, May and June tend to have the highest sunshine averages. The average yearly sunshine for 1980–2009 was 1254 hours.

Climate change

Global warming – the documented historical warming of the earth, based on over 130 years of temperature records from around the world – is often used synonymously with climate change. However, the latter is more complicated than just 'warming' and changes in the amount and patterns of rainfall may be equally important. There is some evidence that climate change is affecting the flora and fauna.

In order to spread, some plant species need a disproportionate increase in summer temperatures as opposed to winter temperature increases. At a UK level it has been shown that native plants are flowering five days earlier for every rise in temperature of one degree Celsius. On average, plants flowered two–twelve days earlier over the last 25 years compared

with any other consecutive 25-year period since records began.

There is little direct evidence that local plant species are flowering earlier than previously, but there is evidence of a warmer climate encouraging trees to set viable seed. Lime seedlings were well documented in the 1990s and seedlings of other southern species, such as hornbeam and field maple, can also be found. Beech, which already regenerates well, may be further encouraged and seedlings of sweet chestnut and small-leaved lime may start to appear; non-native species such as Turkey oak and false-acacia may also be expected to increase.

Some herbaceous plants such as wall barley, common mallow, barren brome, bladder campion, cowslip, great mullein, hedge bedstraw, hemlock, rough chervil, white dead-nettle, wild carrot, wild parsnip and wormwood, which are all currently uncommon in the local area, may spread as a result of a warming of the climate. Such a warming will also encourage the many established and the more transitory non-native members of the local flora to become more plentiful.

Climate change may also bring opportunities for some animal species. Although there have been few obvious changes noted so far with birds and mammals, some invertebrates have responded quite rapidly. There have been major expansions in the range of four butterflies in the area. These are all 'generalist' species – they do not have specific habitat requirements and the caterpillars eat common and widespread plants. Previously rare or completely absent from the area in the early 1980s, the ringlet, peacock and orange-tip are now widespread and common, while the comma has only recently arrived and is starting to spread. The orange-tip has appeared progressively earlier over the last 30 years is now often seen in early April.

Habitats

Around Glasgow there is a diverse range of upland and lowland habitats, including woodlands, wetlands, farmlands and urban areas. Particular habitats provide suitable conditions for different species of plants and animals to live in. Cockles and mussels thrive in the Clyde Estuary, the stag's-horn clubmoss occurs in the Kilpatrick Hills, and ravens in the Campsie Fells, while Michaelmas-daisies (garden escapees) and house spiders are plentiful in the centres of Glasgow and Paisley. The local geology and climate influence habitats – but the impact of humans over thousands of years has also greatly modified the nature of the local landscape.

Woodlands

Much of the area was covered by trees for about 6000 years, but now almost all of the original woodland has been felled. Only small areas of ancient woodland survive, such as at Mugdock Wood (NS 545 765). The varied topography of the area, and particularly steeper ground and watercourse valleys, where there is little grazing, has enabled other woodland relics to survive. Woodlands dominated by ash and elm cling to the steeper ground and are the most important places to find species-rich ground floras and local rarities.

There are also patches of semi-natural woodland, a few hundred years old, which were originally managed, but now have often been left to grow wild. Broadleaved woodlands on the upland fringe or leveller ground in urban areas tend to be much more influenced by past planting, so native trees such as oak and ash are joined by exotic beech, sycamore, horse chestnut and lime, and by other trees including conifers, notably Scot's pine and larch. Non-native shrubs, including the cherry laurel, snowberry and the invasive rhododendron, can be common, but a range of native and alien ground-flora plant species are also present. Wet woodlands can be found on poorly draining areas and along watercourses: willows and alder pick out less acidic conditions and birch grows on peaty ground.

Mugdock Wood.

© Mugdock Country Park

In the twentieth century many conifer plantations were established. Notable areas include the Kilpatrick Hills, the Carron Valley Forest on the northern side of the Kilsyth Hills, Whitelee Forest (to the west of Strathaven) and the Central Scotland Forest to the north-east of Newmains and Carluke. These forests often consist mainly of plantings of one species such as sitka spruce. Many of these monocultures are of limited value for wildlife, as the closely planted trees cast dense shade, preventing the growth of the native plants beneath them. Today, most new forestry plantations contain a mixture of species, including native broadleaved trees. Many new woodlands about towns are 'Community Woodlands' which contain a high proportion of native species and are potentially more beneficial to wildlife.

The impact of farming

Agriculture, mostly in the form of grazing cattle and sheep, has transformed the once wooded landscape to one of improved pasture fields demarcated by hedgerows, stone walls and fences. In common with much of the rest of the country, the lowland grasslands have been intensively improved by better drainage, ploughing and seeding. Traditionally managed species-rich lowland meadows are now a very rare sight. Many of the most diverse grasslands are now to be found in urban areas, where alien species can be frequent, such as at the many old industrial sites along the Clyde in Glasgow, old pit bings and disused railway lines. However, the majority of these lack management and tall herbs or scrub habitats often take over eventually.

Agricultural improvement can extend well into the upland fringes, but further up the higher ground tends to support rough grazing marked by acid grasslands and dwarf-shrub heath. Where not too intensely grazed or drained, this grades into marshy rush pastures or moorlands on deep peats. Some of the most species-rich grassland, and local rarities, are associated with the shallow, often mineral-rich soils of rocky ground, slopes and valley sides.

Uplands

The uplands formed by the Campsie Fells, Kilpatrick Hills, Renfrewshire Heights and Lanarkshire hills provide impressive

The open slopes of the Campsie Fells contrast with the wooded valley of the Glazert Water.

© Richard Sutcliffe

landscape backdrops to the local area. Although true subalpine plants are rare, with a few restricted to the highest reaches (above 500m), the rocky outcrops, burnside gorges, moorlands and extensive rough grasslands harbour a few upland species not found lower down, including lesser twayblade, cowberry, cloudberry, mossy saxifrage, starry saxifrage, parsley fern and clubmosses.

Wetlands

The area supports extensive wetland habitats, due to high rainfall, undulating ground and large low-lying alluvial areas. These range from marshy grasslands and peaty fens through to swamps and boglands and the open waters of ponds, reservoirs and lochs. Lowland marshes, fens and the margins of open water support a rich and diverse variety of wetland species, but on agricultural ground domination by rushes is a common sight. Various grass-like sedges, rushes and reeds form extensive swamps where the water levels remain high all year, and open water bodies and waterways, including rivers and canals, support a range of submerged and floating aquatic plant communities.

Natural rivers and burns create a number of different habitats, and these in turn support a wide range of wildlife. In general, the more diverse the habitats, the greater the variety of species living in them. Modified or engineered water bodies generally result in fewer habitats and support fewer species.

Peatbogs are a special feature of the area with upland blanket mires on the higher ground and more discrete lowland raised bogs on floodplains and depressions on hilly ground. Peatbogs contain heathers, cottongrasses and moor-grasses and a colourful mix of bog-mosses along with other mosses, liverworts and lichens.

Coastal habitats

The maritime influence of the Firth of Clyde affects not only the climate: the tidal reaches and surface spray also create distinctive coastal habitats. Beaches, dunes and lichen-encrusted rock outcrops are restricted to the narrow, western fringes of the area, but extensive saltmarshes and estuarine mud form important resources for invertebrates and birds along the tidal reaches of the Clyde Estuary between Greenock and Erskine. Tidal influences reach all the way up the Clyde to the weir at Glasgow Green, allowing some marine species to get right into the centre of Glasgow.

Urban landscapes

The conurbations associated with Greater Glasgow stretch along the Clyde and its tributaries, and are the product of a highly modified urban landscape covering a substantial part of the local area. However, even in such human landscapes wildlife can thrive. Many urban greenspaces support pockets of former countryside, including grasslands and wetlands, and parks and old estate woodlands can harbour rich woodland habitats. Urban gardens are increasingly a substantial reservoir of plants and associated wildlife. Derelict land, or so-called brownfield sites such as wasteground, disused railways, pit bings and old industrial sites, are often remarkable for the rich floras that have followed from their creation or abandonment.

A derelict brownfield site near the River Clyde in Glasgow, home to a wide range of plants and animals.

© Richard Sutcliffe

25

Ice Age to aliens

Ice Age animals

Throughout the Ice Age, which began some 2.5 million years ago, glaciers advanced and decayed many times as climatic conditions fluctuated. From around 40,000 years ago, during periods when the ice had retreated and tundra conditions prevailed, animals such as woolly mammoth, woolly rhinoceros and reindeer roamed the Glasgow area.

Several woolly rhinoceros bones have been found in sand and gravel quarries near Bishopbriggs. Two of the bones have been radiocarbon dated to 30,550 and 32,000 years old. The only other find of woolly rhinoceros in Scotland was made at Sourlie near Irvine – it was dated to a similar age, and discovered with part of a reindeer antler and the remains of mosses, grasses, sedges and water plants, which indicate that the environment the animals inhabited was treeless with areas of open water.

Woolly mammoth teeth and tusks have been found at several sites around Glasgow and Ayrshire. These date from more than 40,000 to 13,700 years ago. It appears that both woolly mammoth and woolly rhinoceros became extinct in Scotland before the end of the Ice Age, 11,500 years ago.

Pieces of reindeer leg bones and antler from Mount Florida, Glasgow. (Glasgow Museums, nos A.1937.52.a and b)

Reindeer remains, particularly antlers, have been discovered at a number of sites around Glasgow. Part of a reindeer antler and bone fragments were found in 1937 at Mount Florida in the south side of the city, in a layer of sand and gravel uncovered during tunnelling work for a new sewer. The layer of sediment containing the reindeer remains was underneath till deposited by Ice Age glaciers, and so must predate the last glaciation in the Glasgow area, which began around 30,000 years ago. The antler has not been radiocarbon dated but it is probably about the same age as the Bishopbriggs woolly rhinoceros, around 30,000 years old. Other fossils that have been dated show that reindeer lived in Scotland for much of the late Ice Age and just after, between 48,000 and 8300 years ago.

After the ice

Much of the Glasgow area has been ice free for 15,000 years. Studies carried out at the University of Glasgow have helped to give us some idea of how the landscape has changed since the last Ice Age glaciers retreated from Scotland about 11,500 years ago. Analysis of the earliest vegetation samples indicate a developing tundra-type flora, characterized by low-growing grasses, sedges, herbs and mosses with a dwarf scrub of juniper and dwarf willows and birch. The trend was reversed by the Lomond Re-advance, about 12,900 years ago, when the ice-sheet extended southwards, but from around 11,500 years ago onwards rapid climatic warming was underway, and birch woodland quickly spread and soon covered much of central Scotland. Hazel quickly followed and elm and oak were present by around 9000 years ago. Later alder and Scots pine arrived. Scots pine was probably never present in significant amounts in central Scotland, but pine

Iceland scallop from the Clyde Beds deposits. (Glasgow Museums, no. 1902.168.bew)

stumps dated to 4270 years old have been found in local peat bogs; it is believed that pine generally only colonized drier areas of peat bogs.

Reindeer and other tundra species such as the giant Irish deer, arctic fox and wild horse just survived into the post-glacial period, until the climate warmed and the tundra environment was succeeded by forest.

Some of the marine life of the Glasgow area 13,000 years ago, a time of high sea levels, is preserved in clays deposited on the seabed. These clays are not well exposed at the surface and most of the fossil material has been collected from temporary excavations, including during the construction of docks along the River Clyde. The fossil remains are dominated by the shells of gastropod and bivalve molluscs, and there are also fossils of starfish, sea urchins, barnacles, crabs, marine worms and fish bones. The fauna was very similar to that of the present-day Clyde coast, but with a few interesting exceptions. Molluscs such as the Iceland scallop do not occur in the Clyde today but are found further north. This provides evidence that the climate was colder at this point in Scotland's past.

The impact of humans

As with much of Scotland it appears that some 6000 years ago the climate was drier

and warmer than at present, and with little evidence of human impact, a woodland cover is likely to have dominated the landscape. This was soon to change.

In central Scotland the earliest evidence of human impact on the vegetation is associated with the Neolithic, roughly 4000–2500 BC. By the Bronze Age, about 2700–700 BC, woodland clearance was more evident and this increased dramatically by the Iron Age, beginning about 700 BC. At the time of the Roman presence in the first and second centuries, the landscape of central Scotland was probably pasture and meadows with plant communities associated with disturbed ground, with only a little evidence from pollen for arable agriculture. Following the Romans, it appears that there was a return of woodland vegetation at the expense of agriculture; climatic deterioration may have contributed to this.

Since the Ice Age a number of species have become extinct in Scotland and these losses can be put down to human impact from the Neolithic onwards. Factors such as habitat loss – particularly due to forest clearance – hunting and persecution came into play. Remains of wolf, brown bear, wild boar, beaver, lynx, moose and auroch, including those from archaeological sites, together with historical records, demonstrate that they all lived in Scotland in the past. Apart from the auroch and beaver, evidence of these animals has not been found locally, but there is no reason to believe they did not once live in the Glasgow area.

By about the eleventh century onwards there is strong evidence from sites across central Scotland for greater woodland clearance and increased pastoral agriculture. At the time of the Medieval Warm Period in the late tenth to twelfth centuries – considered a golden age in Scotland, when farming became established at higher levels on hillsides than at present – Scotland experienced hot, dry summers and rather cold winters, with average temperatures 0.8 degree Celsius warmer than in the first half of the twentieth century.

The last 300 years

It is not until the eighteenth century that historical accounts and maps provide a more detailed impression of the local landscape. At this time human settlements, although without the large conurbations of today, were extensive and there was an obvious impact on natural habitats. There were plenty of small farms and hamlets and agriculture was widespread, but intensification and other improvements were not well developed. Woodlands, both natural and plantation, were a scarce resource and unevenly distributed.

During the nineteenth century the expanding population and developing industries further impacted on the landscape. By the second half of the century knowledge of the natural flora and fauna was greatly improved – there was some indication of what was common and rare – and writers were becoming increasingly aware of changes and the decline of several species.

Disappearing species

Among smaller mammal species, pine martens and wildcats were still present in the Campsie Fells until at least the end of the eighteenth century. Red squirrels survived at a few local sites until the late nineteenth century. The polecat, once widespread in the area, was last reported in 1907.

Birds of prey were greatly persecuted and red kite, osprey and goshawk all disappeared from the area in the late 1800s or early 1900s.

More than 100 species of plants have become extinct in the Glasgow area since the late 1700s. These include woodland, grassland, heathland and wetland species, arable weeds and some garden plants. The

Honeysuckle.

main reason for their disappearance was the loss of their preferred habitats. Several other species, including honeysuckle in the wild, greater stichwort and ground ivy, which were probably once found throughout much of what is now urban Glasgow, are now restricted to the outskirts of the city.

The intensification of agriculture and increasing urbanization, from the late nineteenth century to the present day, has resulted in further changes to the composition of our flora and fauna. For instance, some insects – especially those that have particular habitat requirements – have declined or been lost from the city as Glasgow has grown and developed, such as small blue butterflies, which were present in Govan in the early nineteenth century but are now completely absent from south-west Scotland. To a certain extent, this is to be expected. The distribution and abundance of different species is constantly changing as habitats alter.

Incomers

Although there have been many losses to the area's biodiversity, other species have turned up naturally. It is amazing how quickly sites can change. For example, in the last ten years at Drumpellier Country Park (see p. 154), buzzards have appeared and are now nesting, as are jays. Water rails are also now found there, and peregrines are nesting in nearby Coatbridge.

Many plants and animals that do not originally come from the Clyde area are now found here as well. Starlings were almost absent from mainland Scotland at the start of the nineteenth century. However, in the 1820s and 1830s they spread rapidly and were soon found throughout the country. By the 1960s they were present in such large numbers in Glasgow that they were considered a nuisance and indeed a health risk within the city because of their droppings. Flocks of hundreds of thousands of birds were regularly seen coming in to roost at dusk, to the railway bridge over the River Clyde beside Central Station and to the Finnieston Crane. For a variety of reasons, in recent years the numbers have declined dramatically.

Collared doves gradually spread naturally from Turkey to most of north-west Europe between 1930 and 1970. This now common bird arrived in Scotland in the late 1950s, and by 1964 the first ones were seen in Glasgow.

Nuthatches arrived in the area in the last few years, having moved northwards, and are now regularly seen at Baron's Haugh RSPB Reserve (see p. 164) and Pollok Country Park (see p. 72).

Several butterflies have expanded their ranges in the area (see p. 23). The recently

Comma butterfly.

arrived comma has been seen regularly around the Hamilton and Motherwell areas since 2007 and there have been occasional sightings elsewhere.

Some species are doing better in the urban environment than out in the countryside. Red foxes are now extremely common within Glasgow, where they can find plenty of places to make dens and where there is a huge food resource for them to scavenge.

Aliens

Some non-native species of plants and animals arrive naturally – unconnected to human actions – but some are brought by people, and these are called aliens. Today there are believed to be nearly 1000 alien species in Scotland. Many of these are found in the Glasgow area.

Red fox with pizza.

A collared dove collected in Glasgow in 1970. (Glasgow Museums, no. Z.1970.97)

© Richard Sutcliffe

American skunk cabbage, Milngavie.

The majority of aliens are plants and the first of these were probably accidentally introduced as arable weeds as long ago as Roman times. With increased trade, seeds may have hitched a lift and been brought unknowingly by people from elsewhere – often transported over long distances on ships and arriving with cargoes. Many alien plants have been recorded from around Glasgow's docks, such as rough bent grass, first discovered outside Meadowside Dock in 1979 following the arrival of shipments of grain.

In the nineteenth century plant hunters brought species from faraway locations, and many were introduced into gardens. Some have since found their way into the surrounding countryside and have become naturalized.

Many species that are widespread today would have been unknown to Victorian naturalists. These include many vegetation communities, plantation trees (sycamore, beech, poplar, willows and

a range of conifers), planted shrubs (rhododendron, cherry laurel, snowberry, dogwoods), and extensive stands of plants such as giant hogweed, Japanese knotweed, Indian balsam, pick-a-back plant, pink purslane, few-flowered garlic, 'Irish' ivy, Michaelmas-daisies, rosebay willowherb and many others.

The first records of some of these alien plants in the area include Indian balsam in 1909, which by 1937 was, according to local botanists 'naturalised and growing profusely on the banks of the Kelvin...'. Giant hogweed was noted in 1925, Japanese knotweed in 1926, and was described as 'everywhere' in 1956, Oxford ragwort in 1965 and buddleia in 1982 or 1983.

The effect of man is particularly noticeable in relation to some salt-

Foxtail barley from the M8 motorway verge at Alexander Park. (Glasgow Museums, no. B.1993.68.532)

Japanese knotweed.

© Richard Sutcliffe

tolerant, mainly coastal plants, which have become established and have spread along some main roads: de-icing salt influences soil conditions and also the flora that occurs there. Foxtail barley is now abundant and widespread along the M8 motorway and reflexed saltmarsh-grass is known from at least 11 sites in Lanarkshire on 'A' roads or motorways.

Many non-native animals were also introduced deliberately or accidentally by man into the area. Rabbits were released in the twelfth to thirteenth centuries, although they were probably not widespread in the Clyde area until the eighteenth century.

American grey squirrels were introduced as exotic pets beside Loch Fyne in 1892. Some quickly escaped and became established in the wild. By the late 1920s they were present on both sides of Loch Lomond and have continued to spread. They are now widespread around Glasgow itself, although still relatively uncommon outside the city.

Many fish have been introduced deliberately to watercourses by anglers. For example, grayling were introduced to the River Clyde, and carp into various ponds and the Forth & Clyde Canal. Discarded goldfish formed large populations in the canal at Clydebank in the 1960s. Ruffe, brought from England by anglers as live bait and accidentally released into Loch Lomond, are now the commonest fish in the loch. They threaten native fish, like the rare powan, by eating their eggs.

Coypus and American mink escaped from fur farms. Several coypus were reported from New Monklands in North Lanarkshire between 1949 and 1958, but were caught or died out. Mink, on the other hand, are now widespread throughout the area and have had a negative impact on populations of the native water vole.

As with plants, a number of alien animals – mainly insects and other invertebrates –

New Zealand flatworm.

have come in though Glasgow docks and, in more recent years, through Glasgow Airport. The majority of these are one-offs and never get established.

Other species have or are likely to become established. New Zealand flatworms originally arrived with plants brought from New Zealand. They have been spread with pot plants through garden centres and do well in Scotland's damp climate. These flatworms feed on native earthworms – often virtually wiping them out in fields and gardens.

The lily beetle, a potentially serious garden pest, was discovered in gardens in the south side of Glasgow in 2002. Such species may become a major problem in the future.

Deliberate reintroductions

It is an offence to deliberately introduce a non-native species into the wild. However, under licence, some once native species have been re-introduced in other parts of Scotland. It is possible that some of these species will come to the Glasgow area. In the next few years we may, for instance, once again see red kites regularly flying over the Glasgow skyline.

The study of natural history

A full description of the study of natural history in the Glasgow area and the discoveries made would fill a whole book. Here we will look at a few highlights and touch on the development of some of the many local natural history societies.

Within the Glasgow area, there has been a great deal of recorded interest in the natural world since at least the eighteenth and nineteenth centuries. This was a time when amateur and professional naturalists alike were able to make many new discoveries. Very little was then known about the distribution of plants and animals, and many species were still not described.

Church ministers were often interested in natural history, and in the Old Statistical Account of 1791–99 animals and plants are often mentioned within the descriptions of the parishes. In some cases there are interesting observations. For example, the Revd Mr Archibald Reid describes how rooks in Greenock picked up whelks and periwinkles from the shore of the Clyde, flew up to about 50 feet above the ground, and then dropped them on to stones to break the shells so that they could get at the edible contents inside.

The study of animals
Many early naturalists were interested in birds. In the days before good binoculars and cameras, the practice was often to shoot any unusual bird in order to have a close look at it and make an identification. As a result, some of these have ended up in museum collections – proof that these birds were indeed present in the area at the time.

Robert Gray, the most eminent ornithologist of his day in the west of Scotland, published *Birds of the West of Scotland* in 1871. His book gave an overview of all birds recorded in western Scotland up to the time of writing. JM McWilliam's *Birds of the Firth of Clyde*, published in 1936, concentrated on

Immature glaucous gull, shot at Kincardine on 27 December 1872 by Dr Donald Dewar, a member of Glasgow Natural History Society. (Glasgow Museums, no. 1880.122.vq)

the Clyde area. (Today, the latest bird sightings by current local ornithologists are published on an almost daily basis at www.clydebirds.co.uk.)

From the nineteenth century onwards there was a great deal of local interest in invertebrates, especially insects and various marine species, including molluscs.

Further notable zoologists from the area include, to name but a few: Thomas Gray, 1820–1910 (specializing in molluscs); David Robertson, known as 'the Cumbrae Naturalist', 1806–1896 (marine invertebrates); Alexander Patience, 1865–1954 (amphipods and isopods); Alexander Somerville, 1842–1907 (molluscs); Alfred Brown, *c.* 1841–1902 (molluscs); JJFX King, 1855–1933 (dragonflies); and more recently RA Crowson, 1914–1999 (beetles).

The study of geology
There were also geological discoveries to be made. Greenockite, a cadmium sulphide mineral, was first described by Jameson and Connell in 1840, who examined specimens found in a railway cutting at Bishopton, Renfrewshire. The mineral is not named after the town, but after Lord Greenock, who owned the land on which it was originally found.

Two other minerals, both varieties of saponite, also have local connections. Bowlingite is named after its discovery at Bowling on the north bank of the Clyde. Cathkinite is named after its occurrence at Cathkin Quarry (now infilled), just to the

Greenockite. (Glasgow Museums, no. G.1977.39.76)

south of the Cathkin Braes

A group of fossilized Carboniferous tree stumps were discovered in 1887 when an old quarry was being landscaped in Victoria Park in the west of Glasgow. These are preserved where they were found – protected by a building constructed around them – and have been on display to the public since 1890 (see p. 54).

In *The History of Rutherglen and East Kilbride,* 1793, the Revd David Ure (1749–1798) made some important observations about the geology of the parishes. He also mentions several plants which he thought of interest.

The study of plants

The study of botany has always been popular. The first proper description of the plants of the area was in *Flora Glottiana,* 1813, by Thomas Hopkirk (1785–1841). This was followed in 1831 by the Revd William Patrick's *Indigenous Plants of Lanarkshire* and in 1865 by *Clydesdale Flora,* by Roger Hennedy (1809–1876). The latter was the only flora of the whole area until the publication in 1933 of *The Flora of the Clyde Area,* by John Lee (1868–1959). More recently, *The Changing Flora of Glasgow,* by Dickson and others, was published in 2000. It lists about 1500 species of plants recorded within Glasgow and describes how the flora of the area has changed over the last 250 years. It was based on 15 years of fieldwork, mainly undertaken by members of the Glasgow Natural History Society.

Natural history societies in Glasgow

Natural history societies have been active in the Glasgow area since the mid nineteenth century. They have encouraged the study of all aspects of natural history and over the years have published many of their scientific papers and proceedings.

On 2 July 1851, nine 'gentlemen interested in the pursuit of natural science', as they described themselves, agreed to form a society under the name of 'The Natural History Society of Glasgow' (NHSG). These first members were the eminent local naturalists of their day, with a wide range of interests including geology, botany, conchology, entomology and ornithology.

The Geological Society of Glasgow was founded in 1858, and since that time it has had a proud history of activity and achievement in the study of geology in Scotland.

Within a few years, several other societies were formed, and some of them eventually merged with the NHSG. These included the Glasgow Naturalists Society, the Glasgow Society of Field Naturalists, the Glasgow Practical Naturalists' Society (later known as the Clydesdale Naturalists Society) and the Glasgow Eastern Botanical Society.

Herbarium specimen of a white water-lily from the Glasgow Eastern Botanical Society. (Glasgow Museums, no. NHBNN.20)

© Glasgow Natural History Society

An Andersonian Naturalists' Society excursion to the Falls of Clyde in 1889.

The Andersonian Naturalists' Society (ANS) was formed in 1885; the members considered themselves very much 'amateur' naturalists, as opposed to the more academic NHSG.

The Microscopical Society of Glasgow (MSG) was formed the following year 'for the purpose of popularising the use of the microscope as a recreation, of affording incentives to students of nature to engage in original research and to give opportunity for mutual aid by means of meetings at which papers are read, demonstrations given and objects of interest examined.'

Microscope slides from the Microscopical Society of Glasgow. (Glasgow Museums, no. NH.1983.180)

The NHSG, ANG and MSG merged in 1931 to form the Glasgow and Andersonian Natural History and Microscopical Society. This name was later shortened to the Andersonian Naturalists of Glasgow and in 1979 became the Glasgow Natural History Society. Today the society is still very active and runs a full programme of meetings and publishes papers and its proceedings in *The Glasgow Naturalist*.

A few other local natural history societies co-existed with the NHSG. The Glasgow Philosophical Society, Glasgow Botanical Society, the original Clydesdale Naturalists' Society, the Glasgow Royal Botanical Institution, the Glasgow Zoological Society and the Union Jack Field Club have all come and gone.

Partnerships

In 1982 the Glasgow Urban Wildlife Group (GUWG) – later the Greater Glasgow Urban Wildlife Forum (GGUWF) – was formed to act as an information exchange between all the various wildlife organizations and individuals interested in the city's wildlife and concerned with its conservation. It acted as an umbrella group and was active until 1998. Since then this role has been taken on by the Glasgow Biodiversity Partnership, who produced

Glasgow's Local Biodiversity Action Plan (LBAP) in 2001. LBAPs are seen as a crucial method for implementing the UK Biodiversity Action Plan at a local level. There are similar LBAP groups covering Dunbartonshire, Renfrewshire, North Lanarkshire and South Lanarkshire.

Paisley societies

The earliest natural history society in the area was Paisley-based: there appears to have been one operating from as early as 1847, founded by Morris Young, Paisley Museum's first curator, although it is not clear how long it was active. The Paisley Naturalists' Society was formed later, in 1892.

One of the main goals of the Paisley Naturalists' Society was to identify, classify and record the wildlife and geology of Renfrewshire. The society concentrated on collecting specimens and producing lists for all groups of wildlife to be used by natural historians working in the area. This work is recorded in six volumes of *Transactions of the Paisley Naturalists' Society*, published between 1929 and 1960. The society amalgamated with other local societies and in 1967 changed its name to the Renfrewshire Natural History Society, and published *The Western Naturalist* for a number of years.

Members of Paisley Natural History Society on an excursion to Brownside Braes, May 2009.

© T Norman Tait

The Paisley Natural History Society (originally the Paisley Museum Natural History Club) was formed in 1968. It meets in Paisley Museum and its main aims are to encourage the study of natural history and conservation of wildlife and habitats in Renfrewshire.

Societies in Hamilton, Motherwell and Dunbartonshire

The Hamilton and District Field Club was formed in 1904, but in 1907 merged with the local photographic society to become the Hamilton Natural History and Photographic Society. The society formed a museum in the Free Library in Hamilton, where it then met. The collections are now in Hamilton Museum. The photographic section became independent in 1924 and the natural history section became the Hamilton Natural History Society (HNHS), and continued until the early 1930s. After a long gap, the society was reformed in 1960, initially as a group within the Hamilton Civic Society, but broke away in 1965 as the HNHS once more. It is still active today.

A natural history society was set up in Motherwell in 1907. It was reformed in 1948, but forced to disband in 1962. The West Dunbartonshire Natural History Society was founded in 1969, and produced several issues of the *West Dunbartonshire Naturalist*. It became the Helensburgh and District Natural History Society, but was wound up in 2010.

National organizations

In recent years, many national organizations including the Scottish Wildlife Trust (SWT), Royal Society for the Protection of Birds (RSPB), Scottish Ornithologists' Club (SOC) and Butterfly Conservation have set up local groups or branches and run meetings and excursions. The RSPB run Wildlife Explorers and Phoenix groups for younger members in the Glasgow area.

National organizations have met in Glasgow on numerous occasions. For example, the British Association for the Advancement of Science (BAAS) held their annual meetings in the city in 1876, 1888, 1901 and 1928. For the 1876 meeting, local experts compiled lists of the known distribution of all flora and fauna in the Clyde area, which were published as *Notes on the Fauna and Flora of the West of Scotland*. One interesting entry refers to red squirrels, which were recorded as 'frequent' from Cadder, Lennox Woods, Roseneath and Lesmahagow.

In 1901 a similar but extended version, *The Fauna, Flora and Geology of the Clyde Area*, was produced. Over a century later, this publication is still an excellent source of biological data for the area. The list was again updated for the BAAS's 1928 meeting, as a card index system, which is now held in Glasgow Museums Biological Records Centre. Today the record centre has a computer database of sightings. We are always keen to obtain more records of all species found in the Greater Glasgow area. If you would like to pass any records on, please contact the records centre – see p. 171.

Joining a society

Local natural history societies and related organizations welcome new members. Most hold indoor meetings in the winter months and run excursions to places of interest in spring and summer. For further information and contact details see pp. 169–170.

Conservation

Today we have a very different attitude and approach to wildlife compared with our Victorian predecessors. Instead of killing and collecting specimens for private and museum collections, present-day naturalists are far more likely to photograph and record the presence of species. The emphasis is on biodiversity (the variety of life), conserving species and maintaining or improving habitats for wildlife.

We are now more aware of losses and declines in our local flora and fauna, notably because of agricultural changes and urban developments, and of the growing need to care for what remains. In order to achieve this aspiration there is an increasing range of conventions and legislation, at international, national and local levels, aimed at protecting and conserving what is left of our natural heritage, which is beneficial for us all.

Biodiversity Action Plans

Following the Convention on Biological Diversity (CBD) in Rio in 1992, the UK Government set up the UK Biodiversity Action Plan (UKBAP) to implement the CBD's objectives – the development and enforcement of national strategies and associated action plans to identify, conserve and protect existing biological diversity, and to enhance it wherever possible. The UKBAP identifies the biological resources of the UK and provides detailed plans for conservation of these resources, at national and local levels. UK Biodiversity Action Plans for the most threatened species and habitats have been set out to aid recovery. At a local level, Local Biodiversity Action Plans (LBAPs) have been established.

There are LBAPs for the City of Glasgow; East and West Dunbartonshire; Renfrewshire, East Renfrewshire and Inverclyde; North Lanarkshire; South Lanarkshire; Ayrshire; and Argyll and Bute (see p. 169 for contact details). These groups are coalitions of statutory and voluntary bodies and interested individuals with the same agenda – to translate national targets into actions at a local level in order to protect species and habitats and improve the overall biodiversity of the area. This is done through Species Action Plans and Habitat Action Plans.

Designated sites

Many wildlife sites have some legal protection, depending on how they have been designated. These include internationally, nationally, regionally and locally important sites.

Special Protection Areas (SPAs) are strictly protected sites for rare and vulnerable birds classified in accordance with Article 4 of the EC Birds Directive.

Special Areas of Conservation (SACs) are strictly protected sites designated under the EC Habitats Directive.

National Nature Reserves (NNRs) contain examples of some of the most important natural and semi-natural ecosystems in the UK. They are managed to conserve their habitats or to provide special opportunities for scientific study of the habitats and species represented within them.

Sites of Special Scientific Interest (SSSIs) provide statutory protection for the best examples of the UK's flora, fauna or geological or physiographical features. These sites are also used to underpin other national and international nature conservation designations.

Regionally Important Geological and Geomorphological Sites (RIGSs) are the most important places for geology and geomorphology outside statutorily protected sites. They are selected under locally developed criteria, according to their value for education, scientific study, historical significance or aesthetic qualities. Whilst not benefiting from statutory protection, RIGS are equivalent to local wildlife sites.

Local Nature Reserves (LNRs) are aimed at public access and enjoyment. They allow people to get close to nature and experience local biodiversity near to where they live. They also contribute to a healthy lifestyle by providing opportunities for relaxing walks in the fresh air in attractive surroundings.

Local Nature Conservation Sites (LNCSs) and *Sites of Importance for Nature Conservation* (SINCs) are designated by local authorities as being of local conservation interest. They are defined in local and structure plans and are a material consideration when planning applications are being determined.

Examples of all of these are represented in this book. Further information about other local sites is available from Scottish Natural Heritage's or local authority websites (see p. 168).

Legislation

There are various pieces of international and national legislation to protect and conserve our wildlife and wildlife sites. The principal ones are the EU Habitats Directive (1992), the Wildlife and Countryside Act (1981) and the Nature Conservation (Scotland) Act (2004). This makes it a 'statutory duty' of public bodies to encourage biodiversity. The Wildlife and Natural Environment Bill (still under consideration by the Scottish Parliament at the time of writing) is likely to come into force in 2011. The Joint Nature Conservation Council's website www.jncc. gov.uk gives good summaries and links to relevant UK and European wildlife legislation.

Numerous species of animals and plants (or parts of them) are protected, to varying degrees, by these laws and regulations. Depending on the species concerned, it may be an offence for any person to kill, injure, take, destroy or have in their possession any of the listed species. Please note that ignorance of the law is no defence. If in any doubt, do not collect.

Voluntary codes for collectors

In addition to the law, there are various voluntary codes particularly aimed at collectors. Collecting still goes on – indeed, it remains an essential part of learning about the species which occur in the area. Many invertebrates and some plants and fungi can only be properly identified under a microscope, which is impossible to do out in the field. The information gained by collecting is extremely valuable, and can aid conservation.

Knowing what species are present in the area is a vital. There is little point dedicating lots of resources to conserve what turns out later to be a common and widespread species. The *Code of conduct for collecting insects and other invertebrates* defines certain activities that should be avoided or restricted but it also emphasizes the need to collect invertebrates (see www.amentsoc.org – the *Code* is within the Publications section, under Online Publications).

The *Geological Fieldwork Code* is aimed at encouraging responsible and safe access to geological sites and collecting of specimens (see www.geologists.org.uk/downloads – the relevant document is titled *GAfieldworkcode.pdf*). Many interesting and important fossils are collected by amateur collectors. The *Scottish Fossil Code* gives information about responsible collecting of fossils in Scotland, what to do with any you find, and where to look for further information (see www.snh.org.uk – go to Publications and search for 'Fossil Code').

Outdoor Access Code

Know the code before you go! Everyone has the right to be on most land and inland water providing they act responsibly. Your access rights and responsibilities are explained fully in the *Outdoor Access Code* which can be downloaded from www.outdooraccess-scotland.com (within the section 'Enjoying Scotland's Outdoors Responsibly).

Waterways and water bodies

The waterways – rivers, canals and aqueducts – form important linear features which act as wildlife corridors, linking the Glasgow conurbation with the surrounding countryside. These corridors are vital to biodiversity: they connect up otherwise isolated populations and allow for the dispersion and migration of many species between different sites.

The region contains a large number of waterbodies, including small ponds and lochs ranging from just a few metres across to the impressive scale of Loch Lomond: 36km long, reaching 189.9m deep and containing about 2,600 million cubic metres of water. As well as these natural water bodies, there are also a number of man-made ones – reservoirs, former boating ponds, and flooded quarries, gravel pits and depressions formed as a result of mining subsidence.

Rivers

There is an extensive system of rivers across the area covered by this book. Numerous small burns feed several rivers that drain into the River Clyde, which ultimately flows into the sea. The River Leven drains Loch Lomond and flows into the Clyde Estuary at Dumbarton.

The River Clyde

The River Clyde is fed by water from most of the area covered by this book, and far beyond. It drains the Campsie, Kilpatrick and Renfrewshire Hills in the north, and parts of the Southern Uplands in the south. It runs for 170km and is Scotland's third longest river.

From its source at the confluence of the Daer Water and Potrail Water at Watermeetings (NS 953 131), it flows north to Abington, north-eastwards towards

Biggar, and north again towards Carstairs before turning south-west until just before it reaches Lanark, where it crashes over the spectacular Falls of Clyde (see p. 166). From here it flows north-west and passes between Motherwell and Hamilton, where the course has been altered to form an artificial loch in Strathclyde Park. In Glasgow, beyond Glasgow Green, parts of its course have been straightened and deepened, and large ocean-going ships once sailed right into the centre of the city. Seagoing vessels can still reach as far upstream as Finnieston.

Further on, the river begins to widen, and it flows west past the sites of many former shipyards. Nearer the sea, the Clyde is subject to tidal influences, and the mudflats along the banks are of international importance to huge numbers of feeding birds. Beyond Dumbarton the estuary widens and merges into the Firth of Clyde.

The River Clyde has been of great importance to people: the city of Glasgow and many other places were founded on the Clyde, and it has probably been a source of food for people for thousands of years. Atlantic salmon were once abundant in Glasgow's rivers. In the early nineteenth century, the confluence of the Clyde and the Kelvin was famous for the many fish that could be caught there. At this time the Clyde even contained freshwater pearl mussels.

Simplified map of the main rivers around Glasgow, the Forth & Clyde and Union canals and Greenock Cut.

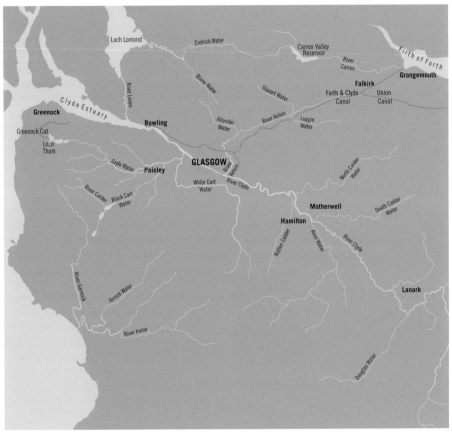

The fish ladder at Milngavie.

The Clyde has been used to transport huge amounts of cargo, much of it goods manufactured in the city's many industrial businesses, and Clydeside became famous for its shipbuilding. As Glasgow grew in population and industry, increasing volumes of sewage and industrial waste were pumped into the rivers. Physical changes to the river, such as dredging and building, also took their toll. Between about 1905 and 1965 the Atlantic salmon disappeared

The tidal weir beside Glasgow Green.

entirely from the Clyde. However, over the last few decades Glasgow's rivers have been getting cleaner. This has been helped by improved sewage treatment, a reduction in industrial waste and clean-up operations. Cleaner water has allowed more sensitive wildlife to return. Atlantic salmon and sea trout came back to the river in the 1980s, and both of these fish now swim upstream every autumn. Fish ladders have been installed on several tributaries, such as one on the Allander Water at Milngavie, making it easier for migratory fish to move further upstream to spawn.

The Clyde is tidal right up to the weir at Glasgow Green (NS 595 643). This marine influence has resulted in some unexpected sightings in the very centre of Glasgow. Seals are seen on a fairly regular basis at the weir – they presumably follow fish upstream – and harbour porpoises have also been recorded here. A common dolphin reached Princes Dock in 1982, and a Risso's Dolphin was seen in 2008. Sea fish such as flounders and mullet have been recorded within Glasgow.

Where the Clyde Estuary deepens, off the Inverclyde coast, porpoises, dolphins and seals are seen on a regular basis and there have even been sightings of a humpback whale on rare occasions.

Rivers running to the Clyde

Some of the Clyde's tributaries have also had an industrial past. The River Kelvin flows from Dulattur Bog, near Kelvinhead, and is fed by the Glazert, Allander and Luggie Waters. Between the Glasgow Botanic Gardens and the Clyde there is evidence of several mills that used to be powered by the river – old weirs and lades, channels that brought water to the mills. In Kelvingrove Park the weirs have been partly destroyed in recent years by the power of the water, and the old mill lade below Kelvingrove Museum and Art Gallery is silted up and is now home to plants such as American skunk cabbage. The staged closure between 1997 and 2003 of old local sewage treatment works, which discharged directly into tributaries of the Kelvin, has greatly improved the overall water quality.

The Friends of the River Kelvin (FORK) (see p. 169) run regular clean-ups of the river. Their logo is the cormorant, which can often be seen flying low over the water, or sitting drying its wings.

Cormorant.

© T Norman Tait

In East Dunbartonshire there are many upland burns running down from the Campsie Fells. These mainly feed tributaries of the River Kelvin, while those originating in the Kilpatrick Hills in West Dunbartonshire mainly feed the River Leven and the Clyde Estuary.

Most of the rivers in Inverclyde, Renfrewshire and East Renfrewshire are relatively short in length. The longest is the White Cart Water, which flows 35km from Eaglesham Moor to join the River Clyde at Renfrew. The other main rivers are the Black Cart Water, Gryfe and Calder. These rivers are fed by a number of tributaries such as the Levern Water, Kittoch Water, Earn Water, Green Water, Dargavel Burn and Locher Water, and some smaller watercourses such as the Spango Burn. There is also a series of burns flowing down from the Clyde Muirshiel plateau. Apart from short stretches of the Kittock, Black Cart and Gryffe, the water quality of most of them is good and supports sizeable populations of fish and other wildlife.

In North Lanarkshire the rivers generally flow across the area from east to west into the River Clyde. The North Calder Water originates at Black Loch, near the village of Limerigg, and the South Calder Water at Shotts. The quality of the South Calder Water has improved dramatically since the closure of the Ravenscraig steelworks at Motherwell.

The River Leven is a deep river and runs the short distance south from Loch Lomond to drain into the Clyde Estuary. It is said to be the second fastest flowing river in Scotland. It is popular with anglers fishing for Atlantic salmon and sea trout, which, along with lampreys and common eels, all migrate up the river into Loch Lomond.

The Endrick Water

The Endrick Water runs from its source in the Gargunnock Hills, south of Kippen, to Loch Lomond. A series of rocky pools to the west of Killearn, 'The Pots of Gartness' (NS 502 866), are a good place to watch

41

The Endrick Pike head. (Glasgow Museums, no. Z.1969.93.1)

© Jackie Gilliland

The Monkland Canal in Drumpellier Country Park.

Atlantic salmon on their way up river to spawn. In 1934 a very large pike, known as 'the Endrick Pike', was stranded at the mouth of the Endrick where it enters Loch Lomond. The Endrick Pike's head is now on display in Kelvingrove Art Gallery and Museum (see pp. 63 and 171).

Waterfalls

The rivers and burns cut through a variety of geological layers, exposing them to view. Where they encounter harder rocks, they sometimes form waterfalls. The most obvious of these are the Falls of Clyde (see p. 166), but there are also impressive falls at the Spout of Ballagan (p. 100), Craigie Linn at Gleniffer Braes (p. 144), on the White Cart in Linn Park (p. 78), at Rouken Glen (p. 150) and Calderwood Glen, East Kilbride (p. 160), and there are six falls in Calder Glen in Clyde Muirshiel Regional Park.

Canals

Canals are man-made water channels which were built in the eighteenth and nineteenth centuries to transport goods and people. They are supplied with water from burns, rivers and specially built reservoirs. Unlike natural watercourses, canals have locks and go up and downhill, which allows them to cross from one catchment area, or drainage basin, to another. In the Glasgow area there are three canals: the Monkland, the Glasgow, Paisley and Johnstone and the Forth & Clyde canals.

The Monkland Canal opened in 1794 and ran about 20km from Calderbank, south of Airdrie, to Glasgow, where it joined the Forth & Clyde Canal. Navigation ceased in 1942. Most of the canal was infilled – the route now lies beneath the M8 motorway – but two sections remain: one runs through Drumpellier Country Park (p. 154) and the other is further to the east near Calderbank. Grey herons, mute swans, coots, ducks and moorhen are a common sight. The canal supports populations of coarse fish including pike, perch and roach, making it popular among local anglers.

Today there is very little left of the Glasgow, Paisley and Johnstone Canal, which was planned as the Glasgow, Paisley and Ardrossan Canal, and built in 1807 from Port Eglington in Glasgow as far as Johnstone. It closed in 1881, and much of its route was converted to railway. A few short sections still remain in the Millarston area of Paisley.

The Forth & Clyde Canal

The 56km-long Forth & Clyde Canal crosses central Scotland, from Grangemouth to Bowling, with a short branch into the north of Glasgow. Built between 1768 and 1790, it was the first sea-to-sea ship canal in the world and served as the 'wet motorway' of central Scotland, linking the east and the west coasts. In its heyday in the 1800s, over three million tons of goods and 200,000 people were carried on the canal each year. Today, 220 years later, this wholly man-made structure is used more for recreation than commerce. The canal is designated as a Scheduled Monument of national importance and is managed by British Waterways Scotland.

Because of the diverse range of habitats, and British Waterways Scotland's low intensity management, which encourages biodiversity, the canal is very good for wildlife. It is host to a wide variety of species, both land and water based, rare and common. The canal corridor includes hedgerows and grassland along the towpath, wetland and aquatic habitats in the canal itself and quieter woodland and scrub areas on the non-towpath side. Even the old canal structures and associated buildings provide homes for some species.

© Robert McLeod, British Waterways Scotland

The Forth & Clyde Canal near Lock 27 between Temple and Maryhill.

Bennett's pondweed and a great pond snail.

© Atom Photographic Agency

More than 310 species of plants have been recorded along the canal. In the summer months, the flowers along the towpath are a riot of colour and very popular with foraging bumblebees. The canal is home to Bennett's pondweed, a hybrid water plant with long twisted leaves, found nowhere else in the world. The waterway is also the UK stronghold for the nationally scarce waterside plant tufted loosestrife, which flowers in July.

Waterfowl are common, and mammal visitors include foraging bats, roe deer and red foxes. The water is teeming with aquatic invertebrates, amphibians and fish, a testament to the good-quality water supplied to the canal from reservoirs in the hills above Coatbridge (via the Monkland Canal, much of which is piped under the M8 motorway). Elegant large red, common blue and azure damselflies are a common sight as they flit over the water surface on warm summer days. Freshwater sponges can be seen growing underwater on the canal's lock chamber walls or on in the canal shallows. They can grow up to 50cm across and look like, on a large scale, flat beige or pale-green biscuits or pale-green beans.

Access to the Forth & Clyde Canal for leisure

The canal and its towpath are used extensively for leisure – for walking, fishing, cycling, running and boating. It is open all year round and the towpath is a mainly level surface; further access information is available on www.scottishcanals.co.uk (or see p. 170).

The canal is linked by the Falkirk Wheel (NS 852 801) to the Union Canal, which, in turn, wends its way into Edinburgh. The canal is part of a network of waterways in central Scotland which connects to the River Clyde at Bowling (NS 449 735) and the Forth at Grangemouth (NS 906 822).

Members of the public are invited to join in the British Waterways' Annual Wildlife Survey – for further details look on www.scottishcanals.co.uk or see p. 170.

There are plenty of places to access the canal along its length between Bowling and Falkirk and Glasgow. The course of the canal can be checked on a Glasgow street map and the Ordnance Survey maps Landranger 64 and Explorer 342.

Three good places to see the canal in Glasgow are at the Maryhill Locks (NS 564 690), Speirs Wharf (NS 588 665) and Firhill basin (NS 582 678).

Maryhill Locks can be reached by a pleasant route along the River Kelvin, beginning at either Kelvingrove Park or Glasgow Botanic Gardens. The nearest train station is Maryhill (Glasgow Queen Street–Anniesland line): from here turn right on to Maryhill Rd and walk about 500m to Cowal Rd, from where you can access Maryhill Locks. First buses 23, 40/40A, 61, 109 and 119 go past Maryhill Burgh Hall, where the road goes under the canal. If travelling by car, follow the A81 (Garscube Rd/Maryhill Rd) to Maryhill and turn left at the traffic lights at Cowal Rd and turn left immediately. There is limited parking available.

Speirs Wharf can be reached by subway: from Cowcaddens Station take the exit for Garscube Rd and walk for 270m, passing under the M8, then bear right up the hill for 200m via a sloping uphill path to Speirs Wharf. Or take First bus 23, 40/40A, 61, 109 or 119 to beside Cowcaddens Station and follow the directions given above. If travelling by car, and coming from the east, exit the M8 motorway at Junction 16, turn right at the traffic lights, go under the motorway and bear left on to the A879 (Craighall Rd). Follow the road for 300m, turn left at the traffic lights and after 170m turn left again. There is limited parking. If coming from the west, exit the M8 motorway at Junction 17 (Charing Cross), turn right at the traffic lights on to St George's Rd. Go under the motorway and then right on to the A804. At the large junction keep straight on, follow signs for M8 East and Port Dundas. Turn left at the second set of traffic lights and then bear left on to the A879 (Craighall Rd). Follow the road for 300m, turn left at traffic lights and after 170m turn left again.

Firhill Basin can be reached by First buses 23, 40/40A, 61, 109 and 119: get off at Queen's Cross Church and follow Springbank St or Northpark St to the Partick Thistle football ground, then turn left and follow signs for the canal. If travelling by car, follow the A81 (Garscube Rd) to the Queens Cross area, where there is limited street parking available.

Tufted loosestrife, with its characteristic paired yellow pom-pom flower heads.

© Olivia Lassiere, British Waterways Scotland

Adult and young little grebes.

Aqueduct
Another waterway of interest in Clyde Muirshiel Regional Park is the Greenock Cut. This 8km aqueduct was built in the 1820s to provide drinking water for people in Greenock and also to power mills. It is fed by numerous burns and runs, and follows a semi-circular route from Loch Thom to the Long Dam (see p. 34). It is now a Scheduled Ancient Monument.

Ponds, lochs and other bodies of water
There are a large number of water bodies in the Glasgow area, many of which are covered in detail in the sites section of this book. They range from oligotrophic (nutrient deficient) to eutrophic (nutrient rich), and the water quality has a major impact on wildlife. A low nutrient content usually means that shore plants are scarce, and those that do occur are specially adapted to nutrient-poor environments. Brother and Little Lochs –about 5km south-west of Newton Mearns – are good examples of oligotrophic open water bodies. By contrast, Loch Libo (see p. 148) is an example of an eutrophic loch – naturally rich in plant nutrients and able to support large amounts of a few species of plants and a wide variety of animals.

© Chris Everett

In the city

Among the many greenspaces within the city are woodlands, formal and country parks, the Cathkin Braes with panoramic views over Glasgow, and some of the best wetland habitats in central Scotland. Kingfishers, bats, buzzards and wild orchids can be seen and there is also Glasgow's oldest attraction – Fossil Grove.

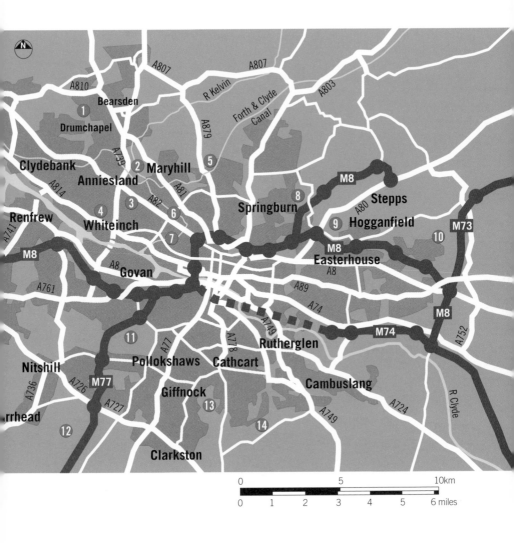

Garscadden Wood

Historic woodland with bluebells on Drumchapel's doorstep

Grid refs: Entrances: Drummore Rd NS 528 721; Peel Glen Rd NS 523 721; Ladyloan Ave NS 518 720

Garscadden Wood, known locally as 'the Bluebell Woods', is one of the oldest semi-natural woodlands in Glasgow. It lies on a steep south-facing slope just to the north of Drumchapel in the former Garscadden Estate, which was established by the Fleming family in the fourteenth century. The Antonine Wall, now a World Heritage Site, runs through the north-west corner of the wood. Garscadden Wood is a Local Nature Reserve and a Site of Importance for Nature Conservation.

The wood consists primarily of mature, mainly deciduous trees, including oak. It dates back to at least 1795 and, as it is situated on a much older site, the core could be the remnant of ancient woodland. There are some trees perhaps 400 years old and there is old coppice and evidence of historical timber management, and also medieval earthworks. More recent planting of native species took place in 1992. The great age of the wood has allowed it to become rich in flowers, including bluebells, wood anemones and dog's mercury.

Many woodland animals are found here. Roe deer can be seen, and also red foxes. Woodland birds include buzzards, kestrels, sparrowhawks and great spotted woodpeckers, as well as smaller songbirds such as tits, thrushes, finches, wrens and dunnocks. The glades in the woodland and the adjacent grassland support several types of butterfly, such as the orange-tip, green-veined white, peacock and small tortoiseshell.

Highlights

In spring the wood is carpeted with bluebells. Garscadden Wood is one of the few sites in Glasgow which supports the purple hairstreak – the caterpillars feed on oaks and the butterflies can be seen flying around the oak canopy in July and August. A pair of ravens can also be seen in the wood; their call usually first attracts attention. They often perch on the electricity pylons at the southern side of the site.

Path through Garscadden Wood.

© Glasgow City Council

© Richard Sutcliffe

Purple hairstreak.

© Glasgow City Council

Bluebells.

Activities

Glasgow Countryside Rangers occasionally run activities such as guided walks – for more details contact the Ranger Service or look on www.glasgow.gov.uk (see p. 168). There is also a healthy walks programme held in the wood: for more information contact Drumchapel LIFE (tel. 0141 944 6004) or the Walk Glasgow Co-ordinator (tel. 0141 287 0963), or see www.glasgowlife.org.uk/healthwalks. Volunteers can help with various woodland management tasks throughout the year: contact the BTCV Glasgow office (tel. 0141 552 5294; email glasgow@btcv.org.uk) or look on www.btcv.org.uk.

Also nearby

Cleddans Burn SINC (NS 509 716) is just 300m to the south-west. It includes the burn itself, wetland, heathland, grassland and recent woodland. The burn is host to water voles and the site also supports wetland birds such as grasshopper warbler, sedge warbler and reed bunting. **Garscadden Burn** SINC (NS 523 709) includes a burn, wetland, wet woodland and mature woodland. The marshes and wet woodland here are notably diverse, with rare plants such as greater tussock-sedge, lesser pond-sedge and fen bedstraw. Water voles can sometimes be spotted near the banks of the burn.

Facilities

Some of the paths are wheelchair accessible.

How to get there

By train: Glasgow Queen Street low level or Glasgow Central low level to Bearsden Station (Milngavie lines). The most pleasant walk is via Colquhorn Park to Chesters Rd and Drummore Rd.

By bus: First bus 40/40A runs along Kinfauns Drive to the south of the wood. Get off near Summerhill Rd and walk north along Summerhill Rd past Camstradden Primary School. Turn right into Bankglen Rd: the entrance to the wood is at the end of this road. First bus 92 runs from Partick Bus Station to its terminus in Peel Glen Rd: walk up the road and turn right into Drummore Rd. The walled entrance is on the left before the school.

By car: From the city centre, take the A82 (Great Western Rd) westwards to the turn-off for Drumchapel, turn left on to Duntreath Ave and continue on to Kinfauns Drive. Turn left on to Peel Glen Rd: there are entrances to the site from both sides of Peel Glen Rd, but the easiest route to the core woodland is from Drummore Rd, the second right off Peel Glen Rd. The walled entrance is on the left before Camstradden Primary School.

Maps: Glasgow street map; OS Landranger 64, Explorer 342.

Dawsholm Park

Woodland and grassland near the River Kelvin and Forth & Clyde Canal

Grid refs: Entrances: Dalsholm Rd NS 557 695; Ilay Rd NS 552 697; north-east NS 558 697

Dawsholm Park is a firm favourite with birdwatchers and general naturalists alike. It consists mostly of woodland and is principally important for the birds that this habitat supports. The park is located in a built-up area, but the River Kelvin runs along its northern boundary and the southern edge consists of three fields managed for their grassland and hawthorn scrub. It is owned and managed by Glasgow City Council; much of the site was declared a Local Nature Reserve in 2007.

The woodland element of the park extends to approximately 14 hectares. It consists of mixed mature trees such as beech, sycamore, oak, cherry, larch, yew and pine; much of it is policy and plantation woodland. Below the trees huge amounts of rhododendron have been removed to improve the wildlife value of the park. The rhododendron and other species, in particular beech and yew, caused dense shading and this restricted the range of woodland plants. However, bluebell, foxglove and wood sorrel are present in areas. The riverbank vegetation is much more diverse and includes garlic mustard, great wood-rush and round-leaved saxifrage.

Grey squirrels are common in the woodland. This North American species does not hibernate and in winter can be seen foraging for acorns or beech nuts hidden in the autumn. If you are lucky you could also come across a red fox near one of the many woodland trails.

A small pond is home to breeding moorhens and mallards, with grey herons also regular visitors. In summer it is a great place to see damselflies; there are three species here.

The Dawsholm Park pond and one of the park's interpretation boards.

© Jim Coyle

© Jim Coyle

Grey squirrel.

© Jim Coyle

Highland cattle graze the grasslands.

The overgrown pasture and hawthorn scrub fields to the south-west and south of the woodland are surrounded by many hawthorn and hornbeam hedgerows. During the breeding season these provide nesting habitat for birds such as willow warbler, whitethroat, wren, dunnock and blackbird. The invertebrates that live in the hedgerows are a source of food for these birds, and in winter the hedgerow berries are eaten by thrushes, including winter visitors such as redwing. Roe deer are also known to frequent this area.

Highlights

Highland cattle were introduced as a grassland management tool in 2008. The results are already proving promising, and it is hoped that this will have a positive impact on butterflies and other insects: butterflies such as orange-tip, ringlet and small tortoiseshell have been recorded. Purple hairstreaks were discovered in the woodland in 2010. The park is also an excellent location to see kingfishers and dippers and these can be spotted from the upper walkway overlooking the River Kelvin.

Activities

There are occasional events targeted at local volunteers or children – for more details contact the Glasgow Countryside Ranger Service or look on www.glasgow. gov.uk (see p. 168).

Also nearby

The Forth & Clyde Canal (pp. 42–44) is about 300m to the south at NS 556 691.

Facilities

A children's play area is located in a large grassed space close to the Ilay Rd entrance, just off Bearsden Rd, and there are picnic benches nearby. Most of the paths are suitable for wheelchairs.

How to get there

On foot or by bicycle: The Kelvin Walkway and cycle path passes the northern edge of Dawsholm Park.

By train: Glasgow Queen Street to Kelvindale (Anniesland line). From the station it is about a 5-minute walk to the park via Dalsholm Rd, but care must be taken as part of this road has no recognized pavement.

By bus: First bus 118 goes along Bearsden Rd to the west of the park – from here you can access the park via the Ilay Rd entrance. First bus 40 takes you to the north of the park, to Maryhill Rd opposite Maryhill Park – get off here and walk down Dalsholm Rd to the Kelvin Walkway and the north-east entrance to the park.

By car: From Glasgow take the A81 (Maryhill Rd). Shortly after passing under the canal, turn left at the traffic lights and follow Cowal Rd and Skaethorn Rd to the second small roundabout – turn right and follow signs to the recycling centre on Dalsholm Rd, where parking is available. Or, from the A82 (Great Western Rd), turn right at Dorchester Ave and follow this road to the small roundabout – turn left and follow signs as above.

Maps: Glasgow street map; OS Landranger 64, Explorer 342.

Bingham's Pond

A green oasis in Glasgow's West End

Grid ref: Great Western Rd entrance NS 554 682

Bingham's Pond is a peaceful open space and a home for waterbirds in a built-up area. Around the site, which is enclosed on all four sides by trees, are Great Western Road, the car park of the Pond Hotel, Shelley Road and Gartnavel Hospital, and the rear gardens of private housing in Whittingehame Drive. The pond is popular with locals, staff and patients at the hospital, visitors to the Pond Hotel and taxi drivers who wait at the stance at the hotel car park. Today Bingham's Pond is owned and managed by Glasgow City Council.

The pond was created in the 1880s on the site of old brick and coal pits. It got its name from the Bingham family, who hired out boats on the pond each summer. In 1956 the eastern end of the pond was sold and infilled, and the Pond Hotel built there. The remaining part of the pond and a small amount of land surrounding it was acquired by Glasgow Corporation for a public park.

In 2003, after the site had fallen into disuse as a boating pond, steps were taken to naturalize the area – to make it more suitable for wildlife. Two islands were constructed so birds could rest and breed in greater safety. Shallow shelves along the edge of the pond were created and thousands of plants introduced. Bulrush, bottle sedge, yellow flag-iris, reed sweet-grass, branched bur-reed, water forget-me-not and purple loosestrife are among the species that can now be found at the pond. As a result, the water quality has improved.

Bingham's Pond in summer.

© Jim Coyle

© Jim Coyle

Tufted duck family.

Five species of waterfowl now breed at the pond – mute swan, mallard, tufted duck, moorhen and coot.

The trees surrounding the pond are of mixed age and type – mainly deciduous but with some conifers. Those to the north and west of the pond stand on an embankment and provide shelter to visitors from strong winds and rain. The berry-bearing trees are popular with winter thrushes, and waxwings have been recorded in recent years (2004 and 2008).

Grey squirrels can be seen in the woodland, coming in from adjoining gardens, and red foxes come out at night. The vegetation under the trees includes bramble and ivy, with bluebells prominent in spring.

Highlights

The pond is an excellent place to see common wetland and woodland birds, and also get close to birds such as the goosander and the tufted duck. This diving duck gets its name from the appearance of the male, which is black and white with a little tuft on its head. In recent years breeding numbers have increased, with a record count of 67 tufted ducklings seen on one day in 2009.

Activities

There are occasional events aimed at local volunteers or children – for more details contact Glasgow Countryside Ranger Service or look on www.glasgow.gov.uk (see p. 168).

Also nearby

The Forth & Clyde Canal (pp. 42–44) is about 1.5km to the north at NS 556 691.

Facilities

A wheelchair-friendly public footpath surrounds the pond. A number of information boards describe the wildlife, and there are two picnic tables and many benches.

How to get there

Entrances: One of the four access points is suitable for wheelchairs: the entrance at Shelley Rd close to the hotel car park. The other stepped entrance points are from Great Western Rd, the Pond Hotel car park and further west along Shelley Rd.

By train: Glasgow Queen Street low level to Hyndland (Balloch, Helensburgh Central and Milngavie lines) or Glasgow Central low level to Hyndland (Dalmuir and Milngavie lines). From the station it is about a 15-minute walk to the pond via Gartnavel Hospital.

By bus: First buses 20, 66, 118 and 159 all go along Great Western Rd – there is a bus stop beside the entrance steps down to the pond.

By car: There is no car parking within the site nor is there any free parking on the streets immediately adjacent to the site. Parking for a fee can be had at the Pond Hotel, or for free in residential areas on the north side of Great Western Rd.

Maps: Glasgow street map; OS Landranger 64, Explorer 342.

Fossil Grove

Glasgow's most ancient site of interest

Grid ref: Fossil house NS 538 673

Fossil Grove, in a secluded corner of Victoria Park, Whiteinch, contains a number of fossil trees of Carboniferous age. These are preserved in their original position – where the trees grew about 325 million years ago, in a climate that was very different to that of today. They represent a natural group of trees, a small surviving fragment of one of the vast, swampy tropical forests of the Carboniferous Period. Fossil Grove is a Site of Special Scientific Interest and a Regionally Important Geological Site.

The fossil trees were discovered in 1887. A small disused quarry within the newly created Victoria Park was being landscaped when workers digging a path exposed the underlying rocks, including the tops of the fossil tree stumps. A careful excavation of the site was organized, which uncovered an area about 23m by 10m and revealed the impressive fossil remains. A building was erected over the excavation, for protection, and opened to the public in 1890 – one of the world's earliest examples of geological site conservation.

Two of the tree stumps preserved at Fossil Grove.

On entering the fossil house, what catches the eye are the large and impressive fossil tree stumps, each comprised of the base of the trunk with its major roots. The largest stump stands about 90cm high with a trunk diameter of 1m. Eight of these are prominent and immediately obvious, and there are 11 in total. Four roots come out of the base of each trunk, and divide into two equal branches. Where preserved, these can be seen to divide again as the roots spread out almost horizontally from the tree. Fragments from the upper parts of other trees, washed into the area from elsewhere, have also survived. The largest is a fallen tree trunk over 8m long.

The fossils are all the remains of a type of tree called *Lepidodendron*, one of a group of primitive plants known as lycopsids and sometimes as giant clubmosses or scale trees. In life, this was a very tall tree growing to more than 30m high. Its trunk was straight and unbranched for much of this length, only dividing towards the top to form a crown of branches. The trunk was not composed of solid wood: its strength lay in a thick outer layer of bark that surrounded a soft pithy interior.

This internal structure was important to the fossilization of the Fossil Grove specimens. After death, the upper parts of the trees broke off leaving the roots and stumps. The soft interior of both soon rotted away and the hollow trunks and roots were infilled with sand. What can be seen today are formed from that sand – natural sandstone casts of the insides of the trunks and roots.

There is a further aspect of the site that is of interest, which dates from around 300 million years ago, a time when the Glasgow area was volcanically active. Rising molten rock forced its way between layers of sandstone, where it cooled and solidified

in horizontal layers called sills. Within the Fossil Grove building, a thin sill of volcanic rock – dolerite – is visible by the north wall, though it thins towards the viewing platform. This sill actually cuts through one of the stumps, showing that it was created after the fossils formed. Outside the fossil house the main part of the dolerite sill forms the rock walls surrounding the building, and the base of the sill and underlying layers of sandstone can be seen beside the pond.

The fossil house, set in a landscaped quarry.

Highlights

Fossil Grove is exceptional in preserving fossil trees at the site where they grew. Within the fossil house, there are also informative illustrated panels about the fossils and the geology of Glasgow.

Also nearby

Kelvingrove Art Gallery and Museum (see pp. 63 and 171) has displays of fossils, including those of clubmosses.

Fossil Grove was excavated in 1887.

Opening hours and facilities

Fossil Grove is currently open April–Sept daily 10am–4pm. For more information phone 0141 276 1695, email LES@glasgow.gov.uk or look on www.glasgow.gov.uk (see p. 168). The fossil house has information boards and a wheelchair-accessible toilet. There are Portaloo-type toilets elsewhere in Victoria Park.

How to get there

By train: Glasgow Central to Jordanhill (Dalmuir line), a 15-minute walk away, via Crow Rd and Balshagray Ave. The fossil house is at the west end of Victoria Park.

By bus: First bus 44/44A runs along Victoria Park Drive North; First buses 204, 205, 215 and 216 go along Victoria Park Drive South.

By car: From the city centre take the Clydeside Expressway (A814 Glasgow–Dumbarton road), which goes past Victoria Park. Then turn right at the traffic lights on to Westland Drive. There is street parking here and on Victoria Park Drive North.

Maps: Glasgow street map; OS Landranger 64, Explorer 342; British Geological Survey S030E Glasgow.

Possil Marsh

A sanctuary for birds with a rewarding circuit around its boundaries

Grid ref: Entrance NS 584 704

Possil Marsh Wildlife Reserve has the shallow freshwater Possil Loch at its centre, surrounded by a ring of marsh, swamp and fen, with areas of wet willow woodland and grassland. It has a long history of being a haven for birds, and was managed as a Bird Sanctuary by the Scottish Wild Bird Sanctuaries Trust from the 1930s until 1982, when it was given to the Scottish Wildlife Trust. Possil Marsh is today a SWT reserve and a Site of Special Scientific Interest.

The site is believed to be a fragment of a system of lochs and marshes which once extended throughout lowland west-central Scotland. The marsh occupies a natural basin between the River Clyde and the River Kelvin, though it is thought that subsidence due to mining activity has also affected the area. The loch is one of only three remaining natural water bodies within Glasgow.

More than 270 species of flowering plants have been recorded at Possil Marsh, including the striking marsh cinquefoil,

marsh stichwort, greater spearwort, common club-rush and the scarce tufted loosestrife. There are extensive areas of wet woodland, with willow scrub carr providing ideal conditions for 'lower' plants, such as algae, lichens and mosses, including the bog moss *Sphagnum riparium*, which is nationally scarce. The woodland contains a range of willows, among them some rare species such as tea-leaved and dark-leaved willows and their hybrids. Scattered hawthorn trees in drier areas provide food for autumn visitors.

Roe deer, red foxes, voles and rabbits can be seen all year round, and springtime brings a perennial host of newts, frogs and toads to the various pools to produce large amounts of spawn.

In autumn and winter the site attracts redwing, and in spring and summer more than 20 species of birds breed here, including reed bunting, grasshopper warbler, sedge warbler, moorhen and the elusive water rail. The marsh also has flocks

View across the reserve with Possil Loch in middle ground.

© Ross MacLeod

© Ross MacLeod

Grey heron hunting.

of common snipe and smaller numbers of jack snipe in autumn and winter. Several migrant waterfowl species appear on the loch, but rarely in large numbers. Great crested grebe and little grebe are among the less frequent visitors. Scarcer ducks which have been recorded include green-winged teal, garganey, gadwall, pintail and shoveler. Long-eared owls occasionally overwinter, roosting by day in dense willows.

The sawfly *Dolerus possiliensis* was first discovered at Possil, in the late nineteenth century by Peter Cameron, who named it after the area.

On the north side of the reserve there is a monument to the 'High Possil meteorite', one of only four meteorites ever to have been found in Scotland, which fell to earth on 5 April 1804, in a quarry near High Possil. The largest surviving piece of the specimen is in the Hunterian Museum, University of Glasgow.

Highlights

The amphibians that are common to the area provide an excellent food source for grey herons, which can frequently be seen standing silently, waiting for their prey to come into range.

Activities

There is a regular open day usually held in June, phone 0131 312 7765 or see www.swt.org.uk.

Also nearby

Millichen (NS 570 720), an area of grassland and arable land beside the River Kelvin that regularly floods, is an important site for farmland birds such as yellowhammer, reed bunting, house sparrow and especially tree sparrow. Large numbers of greylag geese and wigeon are present in winter.

Facilities

There is a circular wheelchair-friendly path around the perimeter of the reserve (2.5km), and there are two disabled car-parking spaces immediately off the Balmore Rd.

How to get there

On foot or by bicycle: Along the Forth & Clyde Canal towpath which is open from Bowling to the River Forth.

By train: Glasgow Queen Street to Possilpark & Parkhouse (Anniesland line). From the station, turn right on to Balmore Rd, and walk north approximately 1km. The entrance to the reserve is signposted on your right, immediately after crossing the canal.

By bus: First buses 7 and 57 go to Possil: get off immediately after crossing over the canal, then cross Balmore Rd, and walk down the ramp on to the canal towpath which leads to the circular path around the reserve.

By car: Take the A879 (Balmore Rd) north from Glasgow. The entrance to the reserve is on the right, immediately after crossing the canal, and just in front of the old Lambhill Stables building. There is unrestricted parking nearby.

Maps: Glasgow street map; OS Landranger 64, Explorer 342; a reserve map is downloadable from www.swt.org.uk.

Glasgow Botanic Gardens

Plants from all over the world

Grid refs: Main entrance NS 568 673; arboretum NS 566 677

Glasgow Botanic Gardens was founded in 1817 by the Royal Botanical Institution of Glasgow. Originally located off Sauchiehall Street, it moved to its current site north of Great Western Road in 1839. The Botanic Gardens has a mix of habitats and displays an extensive collection of plants from many parts of the world. The Main Range glasshouse provides a protected tropical environment, and the Kibble Palace glasshouse a protected temperate habitat.

The grounds contain a wide range of trees, shrubs and herbaceous plants, and there are lawns, a herb garden, a rose garden and an arboretum which extends north along the River Kelvin. The river corridor has naturalized habitats.

The main gardens have some fine examples of trees, including a 200-year-old weeping ash, which was moved from the earlier site in 1841. The arboretum, which is reached via Ford Road or by the Kelvin Walkway, is developing and tree species are arranged in groups: birches, pines, rowans and so on. Many plants here represent the introductions to the UK of the plant collector David Douglas, who collected in North America from 1823 to 1834.

Naturalized non-gardened areas include some of the original flora – great wood-rush and broad-leaved helleborine being just two examples illustrating the former wooded nature of the habitats. Out of a total of 279 different flowering plants recorded growing wild in the gardens, 116 are naturalized aliens. The riverbank areas have a good mix of native and alien species, the latter including giant and hybrid knotweeds, salmonberry, round-leaved saxifrage, purple toothwort and fringe cups.

The most common birds in the gardens are feral pigeons. Wood pigeons are also common. Many bird boxes have been put up in the gardens and these provide nesting sites for a good range of garden species, especially blue tits and great tits. Blackbirds, robins, chaffinches, greenfinches, wrens and long-tailed tits are some of the other species which breed in or around the gardens. Goosanders, mallard and cormorants are found on the River Kelvin in winter, and grey heron and occasionally kingfisher are also sighted here throughout the year.

Tawny owls are frequently heard at night and, although they are not often seen, Daubenton's and pipistrelle bats also occur here.

The Botanic Gardens by night – moth trapping.

© Richard Sutcliffe

Poplar hawkmoth.

The Botanic Gardens by day.

Very tame grey squirrels and red foxes are seen on a daily basis. Roe deer and small mammals such as wood mice and voles are also spotted, but much less often. Insect life is plentiful, with a wide variety of species recorded, including almost 100 species of moth.

The topography of the gardens is of glacial origin. The site, as much of the city, is essentially a drumlin – a narrow steep-sided hill composed of glacial deposits shaped by the movement of ice. Soils vary greatly within the garden but much of the undisturbed soil is clay. Underlying sandstone of Carboniferous age has been exposed in places by the erosive action of the River Kelvin.

Highlights

The two glasshouses, which are listed buildings, hold a very wide range of plants, including national collections of tree ferns and the flowering plants *Begonia* and *Dendrobium*.

Activities

There are regular Ranger-led walks, seasonal tours and special events, for example an orchid festival and a moths and bats night. For more details contact the Garden Office (tel. 0141 276 1614) or look on www.glasgow.gov.uk (see p. 168).

Also nearby

The Kelvin Walkway and cycle path is a quiet and pleasant environment. It goes south to Kelvingrove Park, and the walkway extends north to Milngavie, where it meets the start of the West Highland Way.

Opening hours and facilities

Grounds: 7am–dusk (all year).
Glasshouses: British Summer Time 10am–6pm; winter 10am–4.15pm.

There is a snack kiosk in the gardens and toilets. Although the ground is undulating in places, there is good wheelchair access to the gardens, except for paths leading to and from the River Kelvin. The two glasshouses have wheelchair access, and there are accessible toilets.

How to get there

On foot or by bicycle: The Kelvin Walkway and cycle path runs through the Botanic Gardens.

By subway: The gardens are just 5 minutes' walk from Hillhead Station, at the top of Byres Rd.

By bus: First buses 20, 66, 159 go to Great Western Rd, and First buses 8, 23, 89 and 90 to Byres Rd and Queen Margaret Drive.

By car: Glasgow Botanic Gardens is situated at the junction of Queen Margaret Drive and Great Western Rd (A82). On the site there is no car parking except for holders of disabled badges. Free parking is available on the streets near Queen Margaret Bridge and at the Kirklee (western) end of the grounds on Ford Rd.

Maps: Glasgow street map; OS Landranger 64, Explorer 342.

Kelvingrove Park

A Victorian park with plenty of biodiversity and a museum with natural history displays

Grid refs: Entrances: La Belle Place NS 574 661; Kelvin Way NS 571 666; Western Infirmary NS 565 664

Kelvingrove Park was the first purpose-designed and constructed park in Scotland, laid out between 1852 and 1867. Areas of open grassland are criss-crossed by curving pathways and avenues of mixed trees, and there is a wide range of historic, landscape and wildlife features. At more than 35 hectares Kelvingrove is deceptively large, and although it is a carefully managed city park there is enough greenspace and vegetation to give the site some wild areas and it plays host to a surprisingly large range of species.

Its green slopes rise – steeply in places – away from the River Kelvin, which flows through the heart of the park on its way to the River Clyde, and which is one of

Kelvingrove Park from the University of Glasgow tower.

Glasgow's main wildlife corridors. The river edge is a dynamic habitat influenced by the fluctuation of the water and deposition of sand. The riverbanks are wooded and support diverse plants, including the native ramsons and wood stichwort, and alien species such as giant hogweed, Indian balsam and Japanese knotweed. Improved water quality in recent years has been followed by an increase in the biodiversity of the river. It now supports some ten species of fish, including Atlantic salmon.

Birds such as goosanders, kingfishers, cormorants and grey herons make use of the river, and this is also a good place to watch for dippers. In the summer, sand martins flit over the river's surface, though they nest outside the park boundaries. In addition, although they are rarely seen, otters are present on the watercourse.

© Richard Sutcliffe

Buff-tailed bumblebee – one of six bumblebee species recorded at the park.

The wider park is generally more formal and consists of mature trees, amenity grassland, shrubs and herbaceous borders. Work has recently been carried out to create and enhance wildlife habitats throughout the park. New wildflower meadows and a butterfly garden have been created, which adds to the diversity of plants and provides additional habitat for invertebrates. The park supports all six common bumblebees as well as several species of ladybird and ten species of butterfly.

The formal pond has been naturalized and in the summer there is a colourful display of purple-loosestrife and yellow flag-iris. Grey heron, mallard and moorhen are regularly seen here, and there are sometimes rarer visits from kingfishers.

Small birds feed in the trees surrounding the pond, often coming into view, particularly at the feeders which hang on the other side of the river from the pond, near the band stand. Blue, great, coal and long-tailed tits are all here, along with tiny goldcrests and treecreepers, and the usual array of thrushes, blackbirds, robins and house sparrows. Goldfinches add their metallic song to the chorus, and in late autumn and winter flocks of siskins and redwings often pass through, and sometimes even waxwings. Sparrowhawks are regularly seen in the sky, with their distinctive

The butterfly border attracts insects of all kinds.

© Richard Sutcliffe

Right: Common poppies and oxeye daisies in the newly created meadow.

Opposite: The River Kelvin and University of Glasgow tower.

© Cath Scott

flap-flap-glide flight, while peregrines have been known to swoop on the park's healthy population of urban pigeons.

Red foxes and grey squirrels are both fairly common in the park, both showing little fear of the humans who share their space.

Opening hours and facilities

The park has two children's play areas, one by a well-used skatepark and one at the east side of the park with a café next to it (and toilets for the use of customers or for a fee). Kelvingrove Art Gallery and Museum is fully wheelchair-accessible and has toilets, a café and a restaurant. There is also sometimes a snack kiosk outside the museum between the car park and the river. There are public toilets on Kelvin Way, which runs through the park. The park has an extensive network of wheelchair-accessible paths, although there are steep slopes in some places.

How to get there

On foot or by bicycle: The park can be accessed from the Kelvin Walkway and cycle path, and is only about 2km from the city centre.

By subway: From Kelvinbridge station, exit at the lower level on to the Kelvin Walkway, and follow the river downstream along a path, passing under a road bridge to enter into the park (about 5 minutes).

By bus: First buses 9, 11, 42, 62 pass outside Kelvingrove Museum and Art Gallery. First bus 44 will take you to University Ave: walk to the tree-lined Kelvin Way, from where you can access the park on either side of the road.

By car: From the M8, take the Charing Cross exit (Junction 18) and follow signs to Kelvingrove Art Gallery and Museum. Metered parking is available on Kelvin Way, in the museum car park or in the Kelvin Hall car park.

Maps: Glasgow street map; OS Landranger 64, Explorer 342.

Activities

Glasgow Countryside Rangers hold events in the park and environmental education activities can be booked – contact the Countryside Rangers on 0141 276 0924 or look on www.glasgow.gov.uk (see p. 168). The RSPB runs regular guided walks in the park, mostly at weekends, and wildlife-themed tours and talks at Kelvingrove Art Gallery and Museum – phone the RSPB on 0141 331 0993 or look on www.glasgowmuseums.com or www.glasgow.gov.uk (see p. 168). Practical Conservation Days are regularly held by RSPB Scotland and Glasgow City Council – for more information contact one of the council's Biodiversity Officers on 0141 287 5665/7026. Events are also run by the Friends of Kelvingrove Park and the Friends of the River Kelvin – for more information see www.kelvingrovepark.com and www.fork.org.uk.

Also within the park

Kelvingrove Art Gallery and Museum (open Mon–Thurs and Sat 10am–5pm, Fri and Sun 11am–5pm): the museum has extensive natural history displays, including some about local wildlife, a hive of living honeybees and an enquiry desk where visitors can speak to RSPB officers.

Robroyston Park

Wetlands and grasslands supporting a wide range of bird, insect and amphibian life

Grid ref: Quarrywood Rd entrance NS 629 678

Robroyston Park is a large area of wetland, grassland and some planted broadleaved woodland – some 34 hectares within the urban fringe of north-east Glasgow. The site is noted for its marsh, grass and open-water habitats, which support a range of birds, insects and amphibians. From the park there are good views of the Campsie Fells to north of the city. Robroyston Park is a Local Nature Reserve.

The planted broadleaved woodland is dominated by downy birch with a mixture of other species – such as goat willow, alder, ash, pedunculate oak, cherry and blackthorn – adding variety, which is valuable for wildlife. The grasslands are rich in northern marsh and common spotted-orchids and wildflowers such as sneezewort, meadow vetchling, tufted

Six-spot burnet moth on common spotted-orchid.

© Gavin Finbow

vetch and common knapweed provide an attractive display throughout the grassy areas in the summer. Water mint and lesser spearwort grow in the marshy margins of the ponds. There are a few small areas of heath within the park, consisting of heath rush, cross-leaved heath and various mosses. They also support many different grassland plants such as wavy hair-grass, devil's-bit scabious and mat-grass.

The southern pond at Robroyston is one of the best breeding sites for common toads in Glasgow. Thousands of common frogs also breed annually in both the southern pond and in the larger ponds to the north.

The birds moorhen, coot, little grebe, common snipe, jack snipe and teal are all to be found on the marsh and open water, while buzzard and kestrel are frequently sighted hunting over the grassland. Breeding populations of reed bunting and skylark are also present, as well as grasshopper warbler and willow warbler. The woodland provides cover and food for roe deer and migratory birds such as fieldfare and redwing.

The underlying geology is Carboniferous shales and sandstones with some coals and limestones, covered by till and peat. The park lies on ground restored from historical mine workings.

Highlights

Six-spot burnet moths, which are not common in Glasgow, are found in the grasslands in the summer, amongst the wildflowers. They fly in the daytime, appearing as dashes of colour as they flit from flower to flower. Butterflies such as common blue, small heath, orange-tip and ringlet can also be found in the wildflower

© Jimmy Huls

Robroyston Park, looking south-west over the southern pond.

meadows. Common darter and black darter dragonflies are abundant around the ponds, which also prove to be an ideal home for creatures such as snails, water beetles, leeches and palmate newts, as well as aquatic plants.

Activities
There are occasional events led by Glasgow Countryside Rangers – for more details contact the Ranger Service or look on www.glasgow.gov.uk (see p. 168).

Also nearby
Springburn Park (NS 611 683) is about 1.5km to the west. It includes three ponds that attract a variety of birdlife, including mallard, tufted duck, mute swan, coot and moorhen. Other features are the Springburn rockery and the rose gardens.

Facilities
A large percentage of the paths are surfaced with tarmac, and wheelchair access is good, with most entrances being wide and on even ground.

How to get there
Entrances: There are entrances to the park from Rockfield Rd, Quarrywood Rd and Robroyston Rd.

By bus: First bus 11 goes to Robroyston Rd, and First bus 8 runs from Partick via Parkhead, Provanmill, Springburn and Maryhill to Robroyston Rd.

By car: From Junction 2 of the M80, turn left at the roundabout on to the B765 (Saughs Rd) and left at the next roundabout on to Robroyston Rd. Take the first right into Robroyston Rd and right again into Quarrywood Rd, where there is free on-street parking, or you could also park on Quarrywood Ave.

Maps: Glasgow street map; OS Landranger 64, Explorer 342.

Hogganfield Park

Glasgow's most important site for migrant and overwintering waterbirds

Grid ref: Main car park NS 638 672

Hogganfield Park in the north-east of Glasgow is an area of 48 hectares of grassland, marsh and woodland dominated by the large shallow Hogganfield Loch. The land was purchased by the City in 1920, and in 1924–26 the loch was deepened and an island within it created, which later became a bird sanctuary. From 1930 to the 1980s the loch was a venue for boating. In recent years much work has taken place to enhance habitats and promote biodiversity, including the development of wetlands, reedbeds, ponds, wildflower meadows and woodland – this followed the designation in 1998 of the park as a Local Nature Reserve.

There are attractive plants within the park. Common spotted-orchid, purple-loosestrife and marsh-marigold occur in the marsh area, and amphibious bistort grows in a few places within the main loch. The site supports areas of meadow and acid grassland, with tormentil and heath bedstraw, which are now being sympathetically managed.

Birds are the main attraction of the site,

Adult and juvenile whooper swans.

© Cath Scott

with more than 100 species recorded. Large numbers of wildfowl are present all year round. Swans are very much a feature of the loch: around 100 mute swans are present throughout the year, and they are joined in winter by an increasing number of overwintering whooper swans from Iceland.

Large numbers of duck and geese also winter here, while some come to the loch in summer to moult, when they are rendered flightless. Moult flocks of mute swans, greylag goose and tufted and pochard ducks all gather on the loch. The greylag geese present during the summer are notable – there are more than 300, and most of these migrate to the loch from sites in Gloucestershire. Hogganfield is one of only a handful of lochs in Scotland with a summer moulting flock of pochard ducks. Some tufted ducks ringed at Hogganfield have been recovered in Denmark, Norway and Iceland. Despite the national cull, ruddy ducks are still a feature in the autumn months, when the flock is probably the largest gathering left in Scotland. In 2009 numbers peaked at just ten. Two to three pairs of great crested grebes and up to five pairs of little grebe nest around the loch and there is a small but increasing grey heron colony on the island. Water rail and reed bunting breed in the marsh, while common snipe pass through in autumn and a few jack snipe winter there. Sedge warbler and whitethroat nest in tall vegetation and scrub areas around the wetland.

A number of rare and scarce birds have been seen. These have included black-necked and Slavonian grebes, brent goose, American wigeon, lesser scaup, smew, little ringed plover, ruff, yellow-legged gull, Mediterranean gull and little auk.

Roe deer are often grazing in the marsh and scrub areas, and there is a healthy

View over the pond to the east of Hogganfield Loch.

population of water voles living around the main marsh pond. Common frogs and common toads are abundant, breeding in the marsh during early spring, then feeding in the grasslands during the summer.

Common hawker, common darter and black darter dragonflies, and azure, common blue, blue-tailed, large red and emerald damselflies hunt over the ponds.

Fish abound in the loch. Roach and perch are the most numerous and there are some large carp.

Highlights

This is one of only two sites in Scotland where wild whooper swans have become sufficiently accustomed to people to be observed feeding at an unusually close range – this winter flock now comprises about 20 birds. During the winter you can also get close-up views of goosander, goldeneye and tufted ducks.

Activities

The Glasgow Countryside Rangers run events such as guided walks and special open days. For more details contact the Ranger Service or look on www.glasgow.gov.uk (see p. 168).

Facilities

There is a children's play area in the south-east of the park, sandy beaches beside the loch and picnic tables. Public toilets are available at Lethamhill Golf Course. All paths are wheelchair accessible.

How to get there

On foot: Access points are available from Cumbernauld Rd, Avenue End Rd and Gartloch Rd.

By train: Glasgow Queen Street to Alexandra Parade (Springburn line). From the station it is about a 3km walk to the loch.

By bus: First buses 8, 36 and 38/A run along Cumbernauld Rd, outside the park.

By car: Follow the M8 to Junction 12 and take the A80 (Cumbernauld Rd) north for about 0.5km. Turn right into the main car park, where free parking is available.

Maps: Glasgow street map; OS Landranger 64, Explorer 342.

Bishop's Estate

Three local nature reserves within an area of wetland and grassland

Grid refs: Entrances: Bishop Loch NS 687 664; Cardowan Moss NS 648 674; Commonhead Moss NS 692 659

The name for this area is derived from the hunting estate that once belonged to the bishops of Glasgow. This was a huge tract of land to the north-east of Glasgow, which stretched from the north of the city, where Springburn is now, to Bishop Loch. Today Bishop's Estate refers to a smaller area between Hogganfield Park (p. 66) and Drumpellier Country Park (p. 154) to the east. Much of the land consists of wetland habitat, including several lochs, which were formerly interconnected by a series of ditches or canals. In terms of biodiversity, the area is potentially one of the best wetland habitats in Scotland. A large part of the area has Local Nature Reserve status: the three LNRs at Bishop Loch, Cardowan Moss and Commonhead Moss.

Bishop Loch itself lies in a shallow depression in the land, which is till (boulder clay) left after the last Ice Age. Cardowan Moss and Commonhead Moss are both raised peat bogs, and the largest intact bogs left in Glasgow. They formed where there were once lochs – these slowly dried out and the land gradually became peat bog. The underlying geology is Carboniferous in age, containing considerable shallow coal deposits interspersed with shales, siltstones and sandstones. Various forms of mineral extraction have taken place here in the past.

Bishop Loch is of considerable importance as a reedbed habitat: it is the largest area of reedbeds in Glasgow and possibly the second largest in Scotland. Rare plants such as tufted loosestrife can be found around the fringes of these reedbeds.

Both Cardowan Moss and Commonhead Moss have typical raised bog flora, but Commonhead Moss is significant for being

Cardowan Moss from the bridge over the Cardowan drain – a good place to look for water voles.

© Glasgow City Council

© Glasgow City Council

the only site in Glasgow where bog-rosemary grows. Cardowan Moss includes an area of developing broadleaved woodland with native woodland ground plants.

Bishop Loch has a range of wetland birds throughout the year. Some breed at the site in summer, including great crested grebe and mute swans on the loch, whilst sedge warbler, reed bunting and grasshopper warbler are regularly seen or heard holding territories around the drier margins. If you are lucky you may also catch a squeal from a breeding water rail. In winter small numbers of goldeneye and pochard ducks may be seen.

At both Cardowan Moss and Commonhead Moss a range of butterflies and dragonflies can be seen feeding and breeding in summer. Look out for impressive common hawker dragonflies darting across the bogland.

Common frog.

Highlights

In early May sunshine look for the rare green hairstreak butterfly in the scrubby birch around the edges of Commonhead Moss – the only site within the city boundary where this butterfly is found.

Cardowan Moss is a good place to see water voles, especially along the banks of drainage ditches, or even just listen for the characteristic 'plop' as they enter the water in one of the newly created ponds.

In recent summers corncrakes have been heard calling from the marshes and meadows to the north of Bishop Loch. This secretive and elusive bird is more commonly found in the Outer Hebrides and can be identified by its rasping call, which sounds somewhat like someone running a thumb along a comb.

Bog at Commonhead Moss.

Activities

There are occasional events led by Glasgow Countryside Rangers: for more details contact the Ranger Service or look on www.glasgow.gov.uk (see p. 168).

Also within Bishop's Estate

Frankfield Loch (NS 655 678) is about 200m to the north of Cardowan Moss and can be accessed from just off Cumbernauld Rd. This is a good site to see breeding pairs of great crested grebe. Water voles are also found here.

Gartloch Pools (NS 673 671) are recently formed wetlands on both sides of Gartloch Road, with ponds best known for birdlife. Highlights include gadwall (occasionally

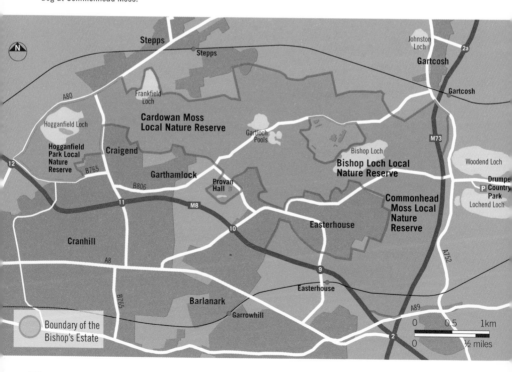

Boundary of the Bishop's Estate

breeding) and gargany ducks, the only breeding black-headed gulls in Glasgow, and uncommon passage migrants including Slavonian grebe, marsh harrier, black-tailed godwit and wood sandpiper.

© Glasgow City Council

Green hairstreak butterfly.

Facilities

At Cardowan Moss there are site maps at the Darnaway St and Avenue End Rd entrances; Bishop Loch has information boards near the entrances off Lochend Rd and Auchingill Rd. Both of these sites are easily accessible by wheelchair. At Commonhead Moss there is currently no signage or formal path access, but there are plans to begin constructing a path through the reserve to Drumpellier Country Park in the east.

How to get there

By train:

Cardowan Moss: Glasgow Queen Street to Stepps (Cumbernauld line). Exit the station on to Cardowan Rd and turn right. Continue up the hill for about 250m and then turn right along Clayhouse Rd, following signs for the caravan park. Continue until you reach the roundabout, then turn left up Lomond Place and follow it to the end: Cardowan Moss will be immediately in front of you.

Commonhead Moss: Glasgow Queen Street to Easterhouse (Drumgelloch line). Exit the station on to Easterhouse Rd and turn right up the hill and over the motorway (M8). After about 300m turn right on to Lochdochart Rd: continue along this, through the housing scheme, until you reach Abbeycraig Rd on your right. Follow this road and take second right on to Allnach Place. The entrance to Commonhead Moss is a rough path immediately off this road to the right.

Bishop Loch: Follow the directions above to Abbeycraig Rd, but thereafter continue along Lochdochart Rd to the bus terminus on Lochend Rd. The entrance to Bishop Loch is right, then first left along Auchingill Rd (about 2km).

By bus:

Cardowan Moss: First bus 43 to Cumbernauld Rd, Stepps. Turn on to Cardowan Rd and then follow the directions given in 'By train'.

Commonhead Moss and *Bishop Loch:* First buses 39/39A, 40/40A and 41 to Easterhouse. From the bus terminus on Lochend Rd both sites are short walks away.

By car:

Cardowan Moss: Take the M8 to Junction 12 and follow signs to Stepps along the A80 (Cumbernauld Rd). Turn right at traffic lights at Millerston (after Hogganfield Park). The entrance to Cardowan Moss is 300m on the left. Parking is available on the opposite side of the road.

Commonhead Moss and *Bishop Loch:* Leave the M8 at Junction 9. From here follow signs for Easterhouse: take the second right on to Lochdochart Rd and then from Easterhouse station follow directions as given in the 'By train' section.

Maps: Glasgow street map; OS Landranger 64, Explorer 342.

Pollok Country Park

A site with many attractions and an ideal place for a family day out

Grid refs: Pollokshaws Rd entrance NS 560 614; Countryside Rangers' office NS 550 616

Pollok Country Park in the south of Glasgow extends over 163 hectares and includes ancient woodland, woodland gardens and formal gardens. The White Cart Water runs through the park, Highland cattle graze in nearby fields and there are working Clydesdale horses in the stables of Pollok House. The park also has archaeological sites of interest, including Glasgow's oldest built roadway, which could date back to 300 BC, and two early medieval ringworks. The land was given to Glasgow City Council in 1966 by the Maxwell family. The council now manages the park, which is designated as a Site of Importance for Nature Conservation.

The woodlands are diverse, with mature conifer areas and mixed broadleaved canopies. Exotic species are found throughout, with beech and Corsican pine plantations to the north and exotic species of oak more southerly, alongside groups of native oak. Yew and holly are regenerating well. Many venerable oak, beech and sycamore are more than 250 years old, with one oak possibly more than 400 years old.

In April to May the woods are full of bluebells. In early spring a rare plant can be seen, especially along the riverside walk: the parasitic toothwort, which has hundreds of spikes in several clumps. Its white scale-like leaves lack chlorophyll and so it cannot photosynthesize, and instead it extracts nutrients from the roots of various trees and shrubs including rhododendrons.

A healthy population of roe deer find a home in the woods and are often seen here during quiet times, and also along the M77 perimeter of the park. Otter tracks and spraints (droppings) can be seen all along the White Cart, although actual sightings are rare. The dashing kingfisher is regularly noted, especially in late spring and behind Pollok House. From October until the end of the year Atlantic salmon can be seen jumping.

Little grebes, goosander, moorhen, cormorant and grey heron are visitors to the river. A pair of nesting buzzards are often spotted in spring and summer, circling the woodland over the fields across from the weir and teaching their young to fly.

In the cracks of the exterior walls of the old stable courtyard there are red mason bees,

Giant hogweed beside Pollok Bridge and the White Cart Water.

© Jim Duncan

Roe deer.

Nuthatch.

Toothwort.

and also their parasite the ruby-tailed wasp. Pipistrelle bats use these buildings too, and Daubenton's bats feed over the water at the lower weir. The wildlife garden pond is home to common frog, common toad and palmate newt.

Highlights

A popular attraction is Pollok's famous heritage beech tree, the Handkerchief Tree. There is a collection of more than 1000 cultivated varieties of rhododendron – many can be seen on the beautiful rhododendron walk.

A new arrival in 2008 was the elusive nuthatch: this is currently the only site in Glasgow where this bird can be seen. Together with great spotted woodpecker and sparrowhawk, it is among the more surprising visitors to the bird-feeding station at the rear of the Countryside Rangers' office, where birdwatchers are welcome.

Activities

There are regular guided walks during the summer, and annual events such a Family Day (early August) and the International Highland Cattle Show (September). For more details contact the Glasgow Countryside Ranger Service or look on www. glasgow.gov.uk (see p. 168). There are graded mountain-bike trails. A day permit from Busby Angling Club outlets allows you to fish at the river.

Also within the country park

Pollok House (open daily 10am–5pm): the Palladian mansion contains collections of

paintings, notably by William Blake and Spanish artists including El Greco.

The Burrell Collection (open Mon–Thurs and Sat 10am–5pm, Fri and Sun 11am–5pm): the collection of the shipping magnate Sir William Burrell, including paintings and objects from many cultures.

Opening hours and facilities

A free courtesy bus takes visitors around the park: Mon–Fri 8am–4pm, every 30 minutes, wheelchair accessible. There are toilets and cafés at both Pollok House and the Burrell Collection, and toilets at Pollok House's old stable courtyard. In general, there is good wheelchair access within the park, and at Pollok House and the Burrell Collection, both of which have accessible toilets.

How to get there

By train: Glasgow Central to Pollokshaws West (Barrhead and East Kilbride lines). On exiting the station, turn left and walk 100m to the main entrance under the railway bridge.

By bus: Arriva bus 3 and First buses 45/45A and 57 stop opposite the main entrance. From Govan and Castlemilk, First bus 34 takes you to Dumbreck Rd – get off at Haggs Rd and walk into the park at the north-east pedestrian entrance.

By car: From the city centre cross the Kingston Bridge (M8) then follow the M77. Take Junction 1 and turn left and then immediately right past Haggs Castle Golf Club. Follow the park road and continue for 1.5km until you reach the riverside car park near Pollok House.

Map: Glasgow street map; OS Landranger 64, Explorer 342.

Dams to Darnley Country Park

A new country park in the south side of Glasgow

Grid refs: Entrances: Nitshill Rd NS 529 596; Parkhouse Rd NS 518 596; Balgraystone Rd NS 506 572

This recently established country park comprises roughly 550 hectares of greenspace, which straddles the East Renfrewshire and Glasgow City boundary and encompasses the green belt separating Barrhead, Darnley and Newton Mearns. It is based around the 'Barrhead Dams' complex of reservoirs and made up of a patchwork of different landscape features and habitats – including open water, wetland and burns, woodland, grassland and scrub – which support a wide range of wildlife. The area is important for its geology and includes a Site of Special Scientific Interest.

In the north of the country park, Waulkmill Glen is an important ancient semi-natural woodland, with ramsons, honeysuckle, wood sorrel and a magnificent carpet of bluebells in spring. It is a SSSI because of the outstanding Carboniferous geology section found within it, which along with Rouken Glen (see p. 150) forms the best outcrop of the Upper Limestone Formation in central Scotland. The Lyoncross and Calmy Limestones are both found within the glen, in addition to a major sandstone, the Barrhead Grit, which forms the spectacular waterfall at the head of the glen. These, together with siltstones and the Arden Coals, represent an area which 320 million years ago was on the edge of a major continent, close to the equator. Unfortunately, much of the geology is inaccessible; the east side of the glen provides the safest route, but the banks are steep sided and have numerous rocky overhangs. Visitors should take great care, especially to the south of the glen.

The grasslands around Darnley Mill are particularly rich in wildflowers, including species such as common spotted-orchid, greater butterfly orchid and cuckoo flower.

The country park contains many miles of hedgerows – mainly of hawthorn and blackthorn – which act as wildlife corridors,

A view north across the dams and towards Glasgow.

© Rick Bolton

Above: Displaying great crested grebes at Waulkmill Glen Reservoir.

Below: Greater butterfly orchid.

© Rick Bolton

joining up habitats within the site and linking them to the wider countryside. They also provide shelter and food for a great variety of wildlife including birds such as greenfinch and small mammals.

The reservoirs are well known for their rich bird life, with over 180 species having been recorded and 45 species known to breed there. The grassland and bushes around the edges support good populations of reed bunting and grasshopper warbler.

Dragonflies and damselflies can be spotted in the summer months. Visit Darnley Mill on a warm summer day and you should see these magnificent creatures flying over the pond or soaking up the sun on the reeds and sedges. In the summer evenings Daubenton's bats catch insects over the surface of the reservoirs, while red foxes and roe deer are regularly seen throughout the year.

Highlights

The greater butterfly orchid can be seen growing on well-drained lime soils, old pastures and in woodland gaps – it is a common feature of the grasslands across

© Rick Bolton

the country park. At night the flowers produce a strong sweet vanilla-like scent.

Common frogs are found across the country park, but can most readily be seen in and around ponds in the Darnley Mill area from March to October. During winter they hibernate underground, in the base of plants or underwater.

Large red damselfly.

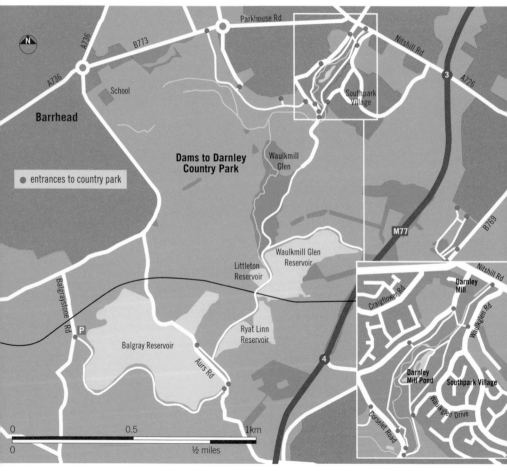

© Rick Bolton

Pairing common frogs at Darnley Mill.

Activities

There are regular events led by Dams to Darnley Country Park Rangers: for more information contact the Ranger Service or see www.damstodarnley.org or www.glasgow.gov.uk (see p. 168).

Also nearby

Glasgow Museums Resource Centre (p. 171) is about 1.5km from the park entrance on Nitshill Road. Tours including the Natural History collections can be arranged.

Facilities

The country park has a network of 10km of paths for walking, cycling and horse riding; the main 'spinal route' and Darnley Mill paths are wheelchair accessible, but there is no wheelchair access from the lay-bys at Aurs Rd. Visitors should bear in mind that much of the country park is working farmland in private ownership.

How to get there

Entrances

There are several entrances into the country park area. The main entrance from the north, at Darnley Mill, is from Nitshill Rd at Corselet Rd, adjacent to the Ashoka restaurant. (Corselet Rd is not a through road and cars should not be driven down it.) Nearby, there are also smaller entrances into the park from Southpark Village – from Waulkglen Rd, via a long flight of steps, Waulkglen Drive and Foxglove Place. Further west there is an entrance off Parkhouse Rd into Corselet Rd. From Barrhead, the entrance is about 500m from St Luke's High School along Balgraystone Rd.

By train: Glasgow Central to Priesthill & Darnley or Nitshill (Barrhead line, with also a few early and late trains on the Kilmarnock line). Both stations are about 800m north of the Nitshill Rd entrance.

By bus: A number of buses go along or near Nitshill Rd (A726) and stop close to the north of the park: First bus 47 stops at Waulkglen Rd; First buses 56/56A and 57/57A stop at Kennishead Rd; Henderson Travel 395, from East Kilbride to Uplawmoor, stops at Nitshill Rd.

By car: At present there are very limited places to park or stop within or near to the country park. Access to the country park from Barrhead and Newton Mearns is along Aurs Rd, but parking is restricted to a small number of lay-by spaces (take care not to block the gates as 24-hour access is needed). Parking is available along Springfield Rd, Barrhead, with access to the country park from Balgraystone Rd. A car park off Balgraystone Rd will open in spring 2011.

Maps: Glasgow street map; OS Landranger 64, Explorer 342.

Linn Park and Netherton Braes

Extensive parkland, gorge woodland and a natural waterfall

Grid refs: Waterfall NS 581 592; entrance to Netherton Braes through Linn Cemetery NS 584 583

Linn Park is a large area of managed parkland in the south side of Glasgow. It includes open grassland, scrub, deciduous and some planted coniferous woodland, and a riverbank environment – the White Cart Water flows through the western edge of the grounds and there is a waterfall, or linn, after which the park is named. Most of the 82 hectares of land was purchased by the Corporation of Glasgow in 1919. Today the park is a Site of Importance for Nature Conservation. To the south are the Netherton Braes, acquired by the City in 1938, which are a major part of the Cart and Kittoch Valleys Site of Special Scientific Interest. The SSSI encompasses an area of mixed deciduous gorge woodland fringing the White Cart and its tributary the Kittoch Water. This is one of the largest areas of semi-natural woodland within the Greater Glasgow area.

The woodland on the braes is dominated by ash, oak, birch and wych elm with a diverse ground flora. More than 300 species of flowering plants have been recorded, including woodruff, wood anemone, broad-leaved helleborine, dog's mercury, primrose and sanicle. Rarities include toothwort, a parasitic plant that grows on the roots of trees and shrubs (see pp. 72 and 73), which within Glasgow is only known at three locations. Badgers, otters and bats are also seen here on a regular basis. It is also an important site for invertebrates.

The White Cart supports a good population of fish including Atlantic salmon, brown trout and other species such as three-spined sticklebacks and minnows. The smaller fish are food for kingfishers and goosanders, which can both sometimes be spotted. Almost 100 bird species have been recorded around the park and the braes, including bullfinch, linnet, skylark, song thrush and spotted flycatcher. Tawny owl, great spotted woodpecker, dipper, tits, warblers and other species regularly breed here.

Meadow at Linn Park and the wooded valley of the White Cart.

© Glasgow City Council

Dipper with caddisfly larvae.

Highlights

The dipper, which is normally associated with clean, fast-flowing upland burns, can be found in Linn Park. Dippers feed underwater, walking along the bed of the river searching for invertebrates and even small fish such as minnows under stones. The birds are often seen bobbing up and down on rocks beside the water. Atlantic salmon jump at the waterfall in the autumn.

Activities

There are a series of events throughout the year organized by Glasgow Countryside Ranger Service and the Friends of Linn Park – for more details contact the Ranger Service or look on www.glasgow.gov.uk (see p. 168), or visit www.friendsoflinnpark.btik.com.

Grey wagtail.

Note: Care should be taken on the banks of the river and on the steep brae slopes.

Facilities

There are public toilets near to Linn Park in Linn Golf Pavilion (NS 578 589). Some of the main paths in the park are wheelchair accessible, although some, including those reached from the north entrances, are fairly steep.

How to get to Linn Park

By train: Glasgow Central to Cathcart (Cathcart Circle and Neilston lines). Turn right outside the station and follow Old Castle Rd, then Snuff Mill Rd.

By bus: First buses 44, 44A and 66 pass Cathcart Station (from here follow the directions given in 'By train'); they also go along Clarkston Rd, past the entrance near Netherlee Rd. First bus 5 goes to Carmunnock Rd, from where you can walk to the Simshill Rd entrance.

By car: Linn Park is on Clarkston Rd (B767): car parking is available at Netherlee Pavilion, off Linn Park Ave. Alternatively, you can approach from Carmunnock Rd (B766): at the large roundabout by shops turn west into Drakemire Drive and then take the second right into Simshill Rd. Car parking is available next to the Linn Golf Pavilion (NS 588 594).

How to get to Netherton Braes

Access to Netherton Braes is presently not ideal. From Linn Park, walk south through Linn Cemetery to NS 584 583, from where there is an obvious desire line through the woods. On reaching the Bailey Bridge, either walk up through the break in the woods or follow the open walkway towards the new weir on the White Cart: just before the weir there is a desire line through the woods. Both routes lead to the former Air Raid Precautions Station (NS 583 575), in the open part of the braes. It is possible to reach this point from Carmunnock Rd at NS 590 583, walking past Mid Netherton Farm along the road to the woods. Direct access to the Braes from Linn Park via Holmbyre Wood is planned, as part of the Magnificent 7 walk: for more information, contact the Glasgow Countryside Rangers (see p. 168).

Maps: Glasgow street map; OS Landranger 64, Explorer 342.

Cathkin Braes Country Park

Spectacular views and varied wildlife on the edge of Glasgow

Grid ref: Car park on Cathkin Rd NS 609 579

Rising to 192 metres, the Cathkin Braes form the highest point within Glasgow, and from the top there are panoramic views over the city. The country park consists mostly of wooded and bracken-covered brae slopes, with plateau heaths and grasslands above, and is one of the most diverse and species-rich sites in Glasgow. The eastern part of Cathkin Braes was gifted to the people of Glasgow in 1887 by Mr James Dick; the Glasgow Corporation later acquired the western part of the site from Castlemilk Estates in the 1940s. The combined area became a country park in 1995 and is designated as a Site of Importance for Nature Conservation, and has been proposed as a Local Nature Reserve.

Skylark with food for young.

Mature woodland, mainly beech, sycamore and oak of plantation origin, forms a central spine within the site, and is the prominent landscape feature; many familiar woodland herbs can be seen here. The northern slopes are more open and support pockets of scrub and remnants of acid grassland and heath, particularly about outcrops of basalt, the underlying rock here. However, they are now mostly dominated by bracken, although this does host spectacular bluebell and wood anemone displays in spring.

Mountain pansy.

The woodland supports a range of invertebrates and common woodland birds, which exploit the mature trees and frequent dead wood. Great spotted woodpecker and spotted flycatcher are regularly seen. The open grasslands are notable for their skylark territories, with small numbers of linnet and reed bunting breeding in the gorse scrub and marshlands respectively. The site supports at least ten species of butterflies, including the small pearl-bordered fritillary, which only occurs at one other site within the Glasgow boundary, at Commonhead Moss. Its caterpillars feed on marsh violets, and possibly also on mountain pansy. There are also numerous moths, including the day-flying six-spot burnet, which can be abundant here in summer.

Highlights

The undulating ridge and shallow soils of the plateau encourage the diverse short grasslands and marshy depressions which characterize the southern part of the site. The grasslands are notably diverse and support many species now rare or absent from the surrounding countryside, along with species such as tormentil, heath

A view across Glasgow from Cathkin Braes.

bedstraw, pignut, bird's-foot trefoil, lady's bedstraw and harebell. Local rarities include mountain pansy, burnet-saxifrage, greater butterfly-orchid, spring-sedge, bitter-vetch, heath spotted-orchid, green-ribbed sedge and heath milkwort.

Activities

There are regular events led by Glasgow Countryside Rangers – for more details contact the Ranger Service or look on www.glasgow.gov.uk (see p. 168). The country park will be hosting the 2014 Commonwealth Games mountain-bike events and a series of bike routes are currently being developed throughout the site.

Also nearby

Castlemilk Glen (NS 608 591) is a wooded area just to the north of the country park, which is fed by north-flowing burns coming down from the braes. There is good footpath access and numerous woodland flowers can be seen in springtime.
Farmland to the west of the braes, which extends from Windlaw across to the Netherton Braes and the White Cart Water, is mostly in public ownership, and has been focus of recent agri-environment initiatives to improve the biodiversity of the farmland. Flocks of overwintering birds and colourful summer meadows can be seen.

Facilities

Signs and waymarks help the visitor explore the main walking routes and there are numerous interlinking informal paths.

How to get there

By train: Glasgow Central to Croftfoot or Burnside (Newton line), both about 2km away from the country park.

By bus: First buses 5 and 75 serve Castlemilk, to the north of the site. First bus 31 stops at Carmunnock to the west of the country park.

By car: The Cathkin Braes lie between the B766 and the A749 linking Glasgow and East Kilbride. These roads are connected by Cathkin Rd (B759) along the southern boundary of the site, where there is a large car park just east of Carmunnock (NS 609 579). Street parking is possible along Ardencraig Rd (around NS 601 584) on the northern edge of the country park in Castlemilk.

Maps: Glasgow street map; OS Landranger 64, Explorer 342.

North and west

West along the Clyde and to the north there are wonderful views of mountains and sea inlets, areas of moorland, the UK's largest loch, a unique fish, ancient woodlands and the remains of extinct volcanoes.

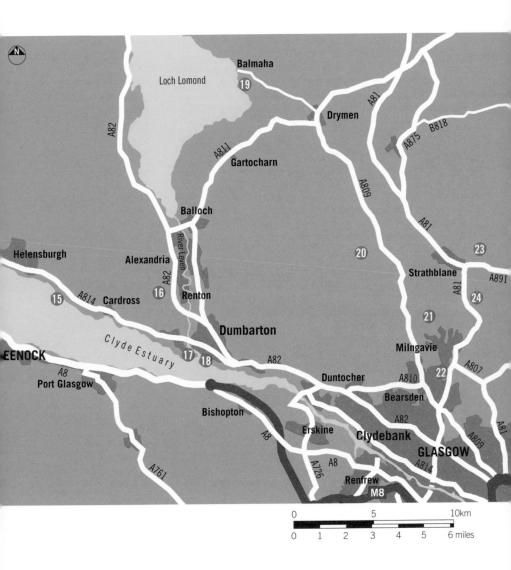

Ardmore Point

A coastal site with interesting geology and important birds

Grid ref: Car parking area NS 324 786

Ardmore Point is a peninsula on the north shore of the Clyde Estuary, between Cardross and Helensburgh. A pleasant coastal walk about 3km long takes you round, and a visit can be rewarding at any time of year. Ardmore has varied habitats and wildlife, and geological features of interest. The underlying rocks are Devonian, or Old Red Sandstone age, approximately 375 million years old. Ardmore Point is part of the Inner Clyde Site of Special Scientific Interest and Special Protection Area, and has been designated as a Regionally Important Geological Site.

Walking around the peninsula in a clockwise direction, it is about 1km before the rocky shore is reached. The rocks exposed on the foreshore are alternating layers of red sandstone and conglomerate. These rocks were laid down as sediment by temporary streams flowing across a plain in a desert environment. The pebbles in the conglomerate are mainly white quartz, with some quartzite and schist – rocks found in the Highlands. Examples of folding and faulting, the result of pressure acting on these rocks, can be found at Ardmore. At one point the layers are folded into an arch shape, known as an anticline. The top of the arch has been removed by erosion but the layers on either side can be seen dipping away in opposite directions.

One of the main features of interest is what is called 'an unconformity'. This marks a time gap – a break in the laying down of the sand and pebbles that formed the rocks. The lower and older layers of rock had formed and then been tilted by earth movements before the upper sediments were deposited on top. The line of the unconformity crosses the shore at NS 312 785. It is difficult to see, but can be recognized by the change of colour in the rocks across it. The older layers to the south are a dark, purplish red while those above are a brighter red.

It is very noticeable that Ardmore Point is on two distinct levels – a wide border of flat low-lying land surrounding a central hill. The change in level is marked by a ring of cliffs mostly hidden by trees. These are old sea cliffs and the flat ground is a raised beach. These features were formed at the end of the last Ice Age, around 11,500 years ago, when the sea was higher in relation to the land than it is today (see p. 19). At that time the sea reached the foot of the cliffs and the high ground formed a small island.

Looking out to Ardmore Point.

Ardmore Point provides a range of different habitats. As well as the rocky shore, there are mudflats, saltmarsh, open fields and hedges, woodland and rough grassland with scrub, gorse thicket and boggy areas. The area supports a rich variety of wild flowers and plants, which in turn attract many different species of birds and insects.

Devonian sandstone and conglomerate with Helensburgh in the distance.

Highlights

Ardmore is probably best known for the birds that come to the surrounding mudflats. The Inner Clyde is internationally important for its overwintering population of redshank and of national importance for several species including eider, goldeneye, oystercatcher, cormorant, red-throated diver and Slavonian grebes. Ardmore is an excellent vantage point to observe these birds, both on the mudflats and out on the estuary, and is one of the best sites in Scotland for seeing large flocks of the latter two species, as well as red-breasted merganser, shelduck, wigeon and curlew. Seals, both common and Atlantic grey, can be seen offshore.

Slavonian grebes.

© David Palmar (www.photoscot.co.uk)

How to get there

By train: Glasgow Queen Street to Cardross (Helensburgh Central line), about 3km away.

By bus: First bus 216: there are bus stops for both directions of the journey at Cardross Crematorium near the Ardmore Point turn-off.

By car: From Glasgow, approach Dumbarton via the A82 (Great Western Rd). At Dumbuck, take the left-hand fork on to the A814 (Glasgow Rd), signposted to Dumbarton and Helensburgh. Continue through Dumbarton and then Cardross. After about 2km turn left on to a minor road at Lyleston Farm. There is car parking at the shore.

Maps: OS Landranger 64, Explorer 347; British Geological Survey S030W Greenock.

Carman Muir

A moorland rich in biodiversity with coastal and mountainous views

Grid ref: Roadside parking NS 374 787

Carman Muir covers 190 hectares between the Clyde Estuary coast and the shores of Loch Lomond. It is connected by woodlands and burns to the Vale of Leven and the nearby towns of Cardross and Renton, though it can still feel remote. There are views of the whole of the Leven Valley, including the Lang Craigs and Dumbarton Rock, and of the Kilpatrick Hills and Loch Lomond. The name Carman is thought to be from the Gaelic 'Cathair Maine', who was, according to medieval genealogies, an ancestor of the Earls of Lennox. Carman Muir is designated a Local Nature Conservation Site.

As the site has a south-facing slope, is near to the coast and has connections with mountainous habitats, it provides good conditions for moorland birds to breed and overwinter. The reservoir itself hosts moorhen, coot, little grebe, goosander, tufted duck and mallard. Sometimes the opportunistic cormorant can be seen here taking a free meal from the well-stocked water. If you are lucky, you may catch sight of osprey, which also fish here.

Other bird species of interest recorded at the site include skylark, linnet, song thrush, red grouse, black grouse, stonechat, meadow pipit, cuckoo, snipe, hen harrier and merlin. Coastal species such as curlew, common sandpiper, oystercatcher and lapwing can also be found here.

The moor has diverse well-managed habitats. Wide areas of wet heath cover the slopes, dissected by acid flushes, dry heath, blanket bog and acid grassland. At various places there are small areas of oak woodland. Although the trees here are small, they are in fact mature specimens.

In addition to the reservoir there are three natural ponds and associated swamp habitat. The vegetation includes common reed, bottle sedge, water horsetail, amphibious bistort, bogbean and marsh cinquefoil. The ponds also attract common blue and large red damselfly, common hawker dragonfly, common frog, common toad and palmate newt.

Carman Reservoir.

Hare's-tail cottongrass on the moorland.

On a warm day, check along the dyke, to the west of the reservoir, for common lizard basking in the sunshine, or look for a stoat bouncing through the grasses. Brown hare can also be found on Carman Muir.

Highlights

Butterflies found on the moor include the dark green fritillary, small pearl-bordered fritillary and small heath. Also look out for the green hairstreak: it always rests with wings closed, showing a bright green underside with a faint line of white spots. It can usually be seen here in reasonable numbers.

There are also black grouse, which are wonderful to behold, although you may be more likely to hear them first. This species is in severe decline and is a high priority for conservation groups.

Activities

There are occasional events led by West Dunbartonshire Ranger Service: for more information phone 01389 737 000 or see www.wdcweb.info. Carman Trout Fishery is available to non-members: phone 07758 725 769.

Also nearby

Kilmahew Woods (NS 353 784), which has native and exotic specimen trees and a lake with dragonflies, damselflies and butterflies. You may see barn owls beside the ruins of Kilmahew Castle. Access is from Carman Rd towards Cardross.

© Richard Sutcliffe

Green hairstreak butterfly on bilberry.

How to get there

On foot: The Carman Muir 100 Steps path goes from Renton through Craigandro Woods to the moor.

By train: Glasgow Queen Street low level to Renton (Balloch line) or Glasgow Queen Street low level to Cardross (Helensburgh line). From Renton Station follow signs for Carman Muir 100 Steps – cross the rail bridge and the A82 footbridge and continue to follow signage. From Cardross Station, go along Station Rd, turn right on to the A814 and take the second road on the left (Carman Rd). Continue until the open moor is reached.

By bus: First buses 204, 205 and 215 stop at the end of Cardross Rd in Renton. Walk up this road to the reservoir. First bus 216 stops at Carman Rd, Cardross. Follow this road for 2km until you reach the open moor.

By car: From Glasgow, follow the A82. After Dumbarton, take the exit for Renton. At the junction with the B857 and A812, either turn right along the B857, go through Renton and turn left after about 800m on to Cardross Rd and up the hill, or turn left along the A812, then right on to the A814, and as you enter Cardross turn right on to Carman Rd and follow the road up the hill. A few informal parking bays are available on Carman Rd.

Maps: OS Landranger 63, Explorer 347.

Brucehill Cliffs and Havoc Grassland

Red sandstone cliffs with ferns and a rich grassland supporting butterflies

Grid refs: Clydeshore Rd car parking NS 390 747; Havoc Rd car park NS 378 754

Brucehill Cliffs and Havoc Grassland are located along the northern shore of the Inner Clyde Estuary. The site, which consists of dark red sandstone cliffs and grassland, is host to an abundance of plant, insect and bird life. It is managed by West Dunbartonshire Council, designated a Local Nature Conservation Site and proposed as a Local Nature Reserve.

© Richard Sutcliffe

Green-veined white butterfly.

The vertical red sandstone inland cliffs at Brucehill represent the former cliff line when the sea level was higher in relation to the land at the end of the last Ice Age (see p. 19). They are almost constantly wet, and the dripping water sustains an interesting floral community, most notably the locally rare royal fern – the largest colony in West Dunbartonshire. The ferns are rooted directly into the cliff faces and their fronds cascade downwards, along with other plants that prefer damp and shaded conditions, such as opposite-leaved golden-saxifrage and hart's-tongue fern.

The upper ledges of the cliffs support a woodland cover of oak, birch, sycamore, aspen, rhododendron and ash. The lower ledges of the cliffs are a mosaic of wet flushes and drier acidic floras. Plants such as heather, hard fern, bilberry and great wood-rush occur in the drier areas. Bluebells are found on the cliffs and under the bracken on the adjoining slope, and are part of the woodland flora.

To the south of the cliffs is Havoc Grassland – a raised beach, another consequence of the former higher sea level (see p. 19). It is an expanse of neutral grassland, marshy grassland, tall wasteland plants and pockets of marsh. The marshy areas support common spotted-orchid, northern marsh-orchid and cuckoo flower, meadowsweet, common valerian, marsh bedstraw and wild angelica. Creeping thistle is present, along with large drifts of marsh woundwort.

The grassland at the site is of relatively recent origin and has colonized areas of disturbance and infill. Growing alongside a wide variety of grasses, plant species include sneezewort, tufted vetch, common toadflax, red clover, meadow vetchling, hairy tare, greater bird's-foot trefoil, common knapweed and the semi-parasitic yellow-rattle. A narrow strip of grassland on the banks of the eastern footpath supports bird's-foot trefoil, St John's wort, hemp-agrimony, glaucous sedge, false fox-sedge and the nationally scarce sand leek. Close examination of the younger, smaller oaks in the grassland will reveal a variety of different oak galls on the buds and leaves.

Plants along the Clyde shore include the pale yellow sea radish, perennial sow-thistle, tall fescue, sea club-rush, saltmarsh rush, sea aster, common scurvy-grass, common saltmarsh-grass, sea-milkwort and sea arrowgrass. Branched bur-reed, a rather uncommon species in the area, is also found here. In some places Indian balsam is spreading and is becoming the dominant vegetation.

Visiting birds include grasshopper warblers in spring, swallows in summer and goldfinches later in the year.

For spectacular views there is an access path that leads you to level grassland at the top of the cliffs. You can look out over the estuary, which is tidal: at low water there are exposed rich mudflats, which provide an important feeding ground for wading birds such as oystercatcher, lapwing and redshank.

Highlights
A large number of butterflies are found at the grassland and in the sheltered areas closer to the cliffs – to date, 16 different species have been recorded.

© Keith Futter

Brucehill Cliffs and Havoc Grassland.

Activities
There are occasional events led by West Dunbartonshire Countryside Rangers: phone 01389 737 000 or see www.west-dunbarton.gov.uk.

Also nearby
Levengrove Park (NS 391 748), a formal park which is one end of the green corridor from Dumbarton to Loch Lomond. Access is from a path along the River Clyde.
National Cycle Route 7 runs northwards alongside the River Leven to Loch Lomond and beyond.

Royal fern growing on the cliff face.

© Susan Futter

Facilities
There is a tarmac path leading down from Firthview Terrace on to the grassland (not suitable for wheelchairs). A more accessible path runs along the shoreline, south of the grassland area.

How to get there
By train: Glasgow Queen Street low level to Dalreoch (Balloch and Helensburgh Central lines). Exit the station, cross the main road, walk along West Bridgend past the high flats, turn right into Clydeshore Rd and walk past or through Levengrove Park. Turn right when you reach the Clyde, and follow the path to the site.

By bus: First buses 215 and 216 go to Dumbarton High St. Walk across the bridge over the River Leven and take the second left into Clydeshore Rd – then follow the directions as above.

By car: Take the A82 from Glasgow, then the A814 through Dumbarton. After crossing the River Leven take the first left (West Bridgend) and then the next right into Clydeshore Rd. Cars can be parked adjacent to Levengrove Park or, at the western side of the site, at the end of Havoc Rd.

Maps: Glasgow street map; OS Landranger 63, Explorer 347.

Dumbarton Rock

The remains of an extinct volcano

Grid ref: Car parking at the base of the rock NS 400 744

Dumbarton Rock is a relic of Scotland's volcanic past – what is left of a volcano that was active around 340 million years ago during the Carboniferous Period. It is a spectacular landform with steep cliffs that rises 74m above the waters of the Clyde Estuary and dominates the surrounding landscape. Its strategic advantages led to the rock being fortified, first in the seventh century; there is still a castle at the rock today. Dumbarton Rock is designated as a Site of Special Scientific Interest.

Dumbarton Rock is a feature known as a volcanic plug. It represents the pipe of a volcano through which lava rose to the surface (the volcanic cone above has long been removed by erosion). The rock is formed from the very last lava that flowed up through the volcano, which cooled and solidified underground in the feeder pipe. Hence it 'plugged' the volcano. The plug is composed of basalt, a common volcanic rock, which can be examined in the cliffs near the road. Here fresh, unweathered surfaces show it is a fine-grained black rock. Looking up at the cliffs where the road goes rounds the rock, you can see

Columnar jointing in basalt.

good examples of columnar jointing. These columns formed when the lava in the volcanic pipe cooled and contracted. Although not so regular, the columns are similar – and created in the same way – as the famous formations at the Giant's Causeway, Northern Ireland, and at Fingal's Cave on the island of Staffa off Mull.

A narrow path around the north side, between the cliffs and the football ground, leads to the shore on the opposite side of the rock (NS 398 745). At low or half tide, you can see beds of volcanic ash (called tuff) on the shore, which are from an explosive phase of the volcano. There are also layers of sandstone and shale. All these rocks

Dumbarton Rock with Ben Lomond and the Highlands beyond.

© T Norman Tait

First Steamboat on the Clyde, by John Knox, about 1820, showing the view downriver towards Dumbarton Rock.

are much contorted and faulted – they fell into the volcano when its centre collapsed, before the plug was formed. Thin veins of calcite cut the rocks.

Dumbarton Rock stands out as such a prominent feature in the landscape simply because the basalt of the volcanic vent is very hard and has survived the elements. It is more resistant to erosion than the sandstones and other sedimentary rocks that underlie the surrounding area. The present landscape has been moulded over many millions of years. Over the last two million years the land has been fashioned by Ice Age glaciers. These ice sheets have scoured Dumbarton Rock into its present outline. Careful examination of the rock surfaces to the side of the steps up the rock will reveal occasional examples of glacial striae – scratches cut by glaciers moving over the rock.

The mudflats around Dumbarton Rock are good for birdwatching. Large numbers of waders and wildfowl winter on the Clyde estuary. Among species that can be seen are redshank, curlew, oystercatcher, greenshank, eider, goldeneye, Slavonian grebe and cormorant.

Highlights
Apart from the interesting geology and bird life to be seen at the site, from the top of Dumbarton Rock there are magnificent views up and down river and over Dumbarton to Ben Lomond and the Highlands.

Also nearby
Dumbuck Hill (NS 421 747), just to the east, is also a volcanic plug, the remains of another of the many volcanoes that were active around Glasgow during the Carboniferous.

Opening hours and facilities
Dumbarton Castle, in the care of Historic Scotland, has toilets, a shop, a picnic area and provides self-service hot drinks. It is open April–Sept daily 9.30am–5.30pm; Oct daily 9.30am–4pm; Nov–March Sat–Wed 9.30am–4.30pm. Entrance charges apply. For further details phone 01389 732 167 or see www.historic-scotland.gov.uk.

How to get there
By train: Glasgow Queen Street to Dumbarton East (Balloch and Helensburgh Central lines). Turn right into Glasgow Rd and take the second left into Victoria St. Continue along this and Castle St to the rock. It is a 15-minute walk.

By bus: First bus 215 to Balloch. Alight at Glasgow Rd near Dumbarton East Station. Then follow the directions given in 'By train' above.

By car: From Glasgow, approach Dumbarton via the A82 (Great Western Rd). At Dumbuck take the left-hand fork on to the A814, Glasgow Rd, signposted to Dumbarton and Helensburgh. After about 2km take the second left after Dumbarton East Station into Victoria St (signposted to Dumbarton Castle). Continue along this and Castle St for 1km to car parking at the base of the rock.

Maps: Glasgow street map; OS Landranger 64, Explorer 347; British Geological Survey S030W Greenock.

Loch Lomond National Nature Reserve

The biodiversity 'hot spot' of Loch Lomond and the Trossachs National Park

Grid refs: Shore Wood entrance for the Endrick Mouth NS 427 877; Balmaha Boatyard NS 419 908

The reserve lies in the south-east corner of Loch Lomond, and consists of the Endrick Mouth and five rocky wooded islands, the largest of which is Inchcailloch. The Endrick Mouth represents the lower floodplains of the Endrick Water, and for its relatively small size it has an impressive range of progressively wetter habitats, from moist woodland, wet woodland, wet grassland, marsh, fen and swamp to permanent open water. The islands of the reserve are cloaked with rich moist oak woodland. The reserve also offers attractive views and scenery.

© Ian Fulton

Greenland white-fronted geese.

© Scottish Natural Heritage

Aerial view of the southern end of Loch Lomond.

The Highland Boundary Fault crosses the northern edges of the islands of Inchcailloch and Creinch and runs to the immediate north of Conic Hill above Balmaha. Much of Inchcailloch and Conic Hill is formed from a large pebbled conglomerate of Devonian age, deposited more than 400 million years ago by rivers flowing down from ancient mountains to the north.

Towards the southern edge of Shore Wood there is a prominent raised cliff line that was cut by a relatively higher sea level, which peaked about 6500 years ago.

It is also a reminder that at this time Loch Lomond was part of Scotland's west coast.

The impressive range of habitats, particularly the Endrick Mouth's wetland habitats, supports many wetland plant species, which reach their flowering peak in June and July and which are alive with insects. They include several nationally rare and scarce plants such as tufted loosestrife, cowbane and Scottish dock. This is the only location for the latter plant in the UK. The oak woodlands of the islands have a good variety of tree species including elm and aspen, and rich carpets of mosses, liverworts and lichens.

The reserve's freshwater is teeming with life, including some notable fish: it is one of only two locations for powan in the UK and also hosts all three lamprey species, including the Endrick's very own small form of river lamprey, with a unique life history pattern. Evidence suggests that the otter population is a healthy one.

© Dr Colin Bean

Dwarf river lamprey.

© Tim Jacobs/SNH

Bluebells in Shore Wood.

Facilities

There are public toilets in Balmaha, Drymen and Balloch. The Endrick Mouth has a path starting in Gartocharn. Inchcailloch has paths, toilets and a Ranger base. Larger groups should phone ahead, and booking is essential for the small campsite – contact the National Park Centre, Balmaha (tel. 01389 722 100, www.lochlomond-trossachs. org). Also use these contact details for booking the solar boat, which may be available for visitors with special needs wanting to go to Inchcailloch, if booked well in advance. For more details about accessibility see www.nnr-scotland.org.uk.

How to get there

On foot: For the Endrick Mouth follow the Aber Path to the Shore Wood entrance of the NNR. This starts from the Millennium Hall car park, Gartocharn (NS 428 863).

By boat: For Inchcailloch take one of the ferries from the Balmaha Boatyard (tel. 01360 870 214, www.balmahaboatyard.co.uk).

By train and bus: Glasgow Queen Street low level to Balloch. For the Endrick Mouth take a bus from Balloch station to Gartocharn. It is a 5-minute walk to the start of the Aber Path at the Millennium Hall. For Inchcailloch take the bus from Balloch station to Drymen, where you may need to change for Balmaha. It is a 5-minute walk from here to the ferry.

By car: Take the A809 Glasgow–Drymen road. For the Endrick Mouth, take the A811 towards Balloch, 1km after Croftamie. As you enter Gartocharn, take the first road on the right which leads to the Millennium Hall car park. For Inchcailloch carry on to Drymen and take the B837 on the left towards Rowardennan. There is a large car park as you enter Balmaha.

Maps: OS Landranger 56, Explorer 347; a site map and leaflets giving directions can be downloaded from www.nnr-scotland.org.uk.

Highlights

From spring to autumn, migrant warblers, redstarts and the occasional pied flycatcher can be seen. Osprey also regularly fish across the shallow waters of the Endrick Mouth and become more active when they have young to feed, from late May until September. In the autumn waterfowl such as wigeon, teal, goldeneye and whooper swans come to the Endrick Mouth, and great skeins of pink-footed and greylag geese often provide a fabulous spectacle when coming in to roost or when leaving at daybreak. A small flock of Greenland white-fronted geese returns to this part of the reserve every winter.

Activities

Occasional events and activities related to birds and summer flowers take place at the site. There are also opportunities for volunteering – usually practical tasks for pond and scrub management. For more information phone SNH 01786 450 362 or see www.nnr-scotland.org.uk.

Also nearby

Balloch Castle Country Park (NS 395 830) is about 6km from Gartocharn. Its designed landscape on the shores of Loch Lomond includes gardens, woods and meadows. The grassland supports numerous butterflies in the summer.

Queen's View and the Whangie

Stunning views, a geological feature and moorland wildlife

Grid refs: Car park NS 510 808; the Whangie NS 493 807

Queen's View and the Whangie are both situated on the northern edge of the Kilpatrick Hills. Queen's View is a raised area at the southern end of Stockie Muir. It was given its name after a visit by Queen Victoria in 1879, as it is where she gained her first sighting of Loch Lomond. Indeed, from this spot you get excellent views of not just Loch Lomond, but also Ben Lomond and the Arrochar Alps to the north. The Whangie is a striking landscape feature about two kilometres to the west, on the western edge of Auchineden Hill. A huge block of basalt has broken away from the hillside to leave a striking narrow chasm roughly 100m long and with steep sides reaching 15m high, which is much loved by rock climbers. 'Whang' in Scots means 'thick slice'.

A variety of explanations have been suggested for how the Whangie was formed, both natural and supernatural. Local folklore claims that the devil flew over the spot, and while doing so flicked his tail

and cut through the rock. It has also been attributed to earthquakes and to 'glacial plucking', meaning that a slow-moving ice sheet passing over the hill pulled the rock away from the hillside. However, the feature seems to be the result of a landslide. The block of basalt split away and slid downhill over weaker underlying sandstones. Older collapsed blocks can be seen just downslope.

Stretching out to the north is Stockie Muir. Here there is typical moorland flora with heather, bracken, bilberry and rowans. In damp areas there are occasional patches of bog asphodel, which has yellow flowers in summer and striking orange-coloured seed heads in autumn.

Ravens nest amongst rocky outcrops in the area and they can often be seen and heard flying overhead. Both red and black grouse are present, and the distinctive 'cour-lee' call of the curlew is often heard. Whinchats, regular summer visitors from Africa, can be spotted sitting at the top of

The Whangie.

Blackcocks lekking.

Bog asphodel in autumn.

isolated gorse bushes. Brown hares may be seen, but you are less likely to spot the more secretive otters, which unfortunately sometimes fall victim to traffic on the nearby main road.

On sunny days in late spring and early summer, several species of butterflies may be observed, including green hairstreak and small pearl-bordered fritillary, and golden-ringed dragonflies may be seen hunting for smaller insects. If you look carefully, the distinctive caterpillars of drinker moths and emperor moths can sometimes be found on vegetation beside the path.

Highlights

If you visit in the early morning, you may be lucky enough to see black grouse lekking – engaged in courtship displays –

Drinker moth caterpillar.

on a mown area of Stockie Muir, which is used by model aircraft enthusiasts, a few hundred metres north of the car park. The males – blackcocks – strut around and try to outdo each, fluffing up their white tail feathers, and making a distinctive call – a dove-like, rolling 'coo' with a regular and explosive 'sneeze', while the females – greyhens – watch from the sidelines.

Also nearby

Auchineden Hill (NS 494 804): there is a path to the top of the hill from the Whangie. On a good day there are fine views across to the Kilpatrick Hills, Dumgoyne, Loch Lomond, Ben Lomond and the Arrochar Alps.

Note: There is a well-marked path from the Queen's View car park to the Whangie. The path is steep in places and often wet and muddy. Walking boots are highly advisable. Allow an hour and a half for the 4km walk there and back.

How to get there

By bus: There is very little public transport, but Aberfoyle Coaches service C8 runs past Queen's View on a Saturday, twice in each direction between Glasgow Buchanan Bus Station and Balfron (see www.aberfoylecoaches.com).

By car: Head out of Glasgow on the A82. At Anniesland Cross, turn right along the A739 and then follow the A809 (for Drymen). Queen's View car park is on the left, about 1km past the Auchengillan Outdoor Centre.

Maps: OS Landranger 64, Explorer 347; British Geological Survey S30E Glasgow.

Mugdock Country Park

A step into the wild on the northern edge of Glasgow

Grid refs: Visitor centre NS 546 780; Drumclog Moor car park NS 554 760; Kyber car park NS 542 774

Mugdock Country Park is situated in a large area of very attractive accessible countryside between Glasgow to the south and the Campsie Fells to the north. The park covers 255 hectares and the primary attraction lies in the quality and variety of its outdoor environments. These range from outstanding natural areas, such as ancient native woodland, open heathland, acid grassland, fen carr and swamp and mire to historically important designed landscapes featuring picturesque lochs and ponds, specimen trees and formal gardens. The West Highland Way winds through the south of the park and the ruins of Mugdock Castle, founded in the fourteenth century, stand near the centre. Some 170 hectares, including Mugdock Wood, are designated as a Site of Special Scientific Interest.

Mugdock Wood is an unusually large area of ancient deciduous wet woodland on a south-facing hillside. It is enclosed by ancient boundary walls, and consists of a patchwork of oak, ash, wet alder and boggy birch woodlands interspersed with bracken glades, grassland flushes, swamps and mires. There are a few formal paths through the wood, but to really experience this wild place it is best to step off the path into a world of huge gnarled trees, fallen oaks, thickets of blackthorn and bird cherry, tumbling burns and boggy sedge-filled marshes.

There is evidence that the wood has been managed since at least the eighteenth century, and visitors can see a variety of ancient coppice stools (the roots and stumps left as a result of cutting trees down to just above ground level at regular intervals to harvest young stems). The coppiced alder are an impressive sight, being multi-stemmed, unusually tall and very well grown. Large amounts of fallen and standing dead wood ensure a healthy invertebrate population: notable species include the leaf-beetles *Phyllobrotica quadrimaculata* and *Pipiza austriaca*, the flea-beetle *Baltica ericeti* and the shield-bug *Zicrona coerulea*.

Drumclog Moor, a 67-hectare area of heather-dominated dry heath, birch woodland and grassland, adjoins Mugdock Wood to the south. It has great views over

Drumclog Moor within Mugdock Country Park.

© Mugdock Country Park

Milngavie and Bearsden, and is home to common lizard, the small pearl-bordered fritillary butterfly and the plants small cranberry, small cow-wheat and globeflower.

The northern section of the park is dominated by grasslands and open water. The grasslands provide good hunting habitat for owls: barn, tawny, long-eared and short-eared have all been recorded.

Mugdock Wood.

At Mugdock Loch, grey herons, cormorants, goldeneye, goosander and tufted duck are a common sight. Huge numbers of common toadlets emerge in late July and cover the surrounding pathways.

Highlights

The nationally scarce, yellow water-lily grows in abundance in Mugdock Loch.

Activities

East Dunbartonshire and Mugdock Country Park Ranger Service runs an extensive range of countryside events: for more details phone 0141 956 6586, email rangers@mugdock.org or see www.mugdock-country-park.org.uk.

Also nearby

Dumbrock Loch Meadows SSSI (NS 548 782), across the road from the park visitor centre, is botanically rich and noted for its variety of orchids and the annual visit of a great grey shrike.

Male goldeneye.

Opening hours and facilities

The visitor centre is open daily 9am–5pm, and houses a tearoom, gallery and gift shop as well as the park reception and the countryside ranger base (tel. 0141 956 6100/6586). The car park and toilets are open April–Sept daily 9am–9pm, Oct–March daily 9am–6.30pm. There is a children's playground and adventure trail. Close by in the walled garden there is a garden centre with restaurant and farm shop. The buildings are wheelchair accessible, as are parts of the park.

How to get there

By train: Glasgow Central low level or Glasgow Queen Street low level to Milngavie, 4.5km to the south of the visitor centre. From the station walk or cycle following the West Highland Way. Leave the WHW when you reach Mugdock Wood and follow signs.

By bus: The park is served by MyBus Rural buses 600 and 850, which provide transport where there is no alternative public transport available: to book phone 0845 128 4037 or see www.spt.co.uk.

By car: From Glasgow take the A81 (Aberfoyle road) north through Bearsden and Milngavie. Mugdock Country Park is signposted from Milngavie. After about 3km, turn left off the A81 and continue to follow the signs. There are five free car parks around the park.

Maps: OS Landranger 64, Explorer 348; a park map can be downloaded from www.mugdock-country-park.org.uk.

Kilmardinny Loch

A wildlife haven in a suburban setting

Grid refs: Kilmardinny Ave entrance NS 551 729; Thomson Drive entrance NS 547 729

Kilmardinny Loch lies at the centre of what remains of the former eighteenth- and nineteenth-century Kilmardinny Estate. The area around the loch is a public park, mainly enclosed by semi-natural, broadleaved woodland, with some areas of amenity grassland, and is a haven for wildlife surrounded by housing. The site is designated as a Local Nature Reserve.

The loch itself is believed to be what is known as a 'kettle hole'. It was formed at the end of the last Ice Age, about 11,500 years ago, when a large chunk of ice became detached from a retreating glacier. Sediments from meltwater then built up around the block of ice. When the ice eventually all melted, it left behind a depression, which filled with water, forming the loch. The nearby, inaccessible, St Germains Loch probably also formed in this way.

Parts of the loch are choked with water-lilies in the summer. They are all the hybrid water-lily *Nuphar x spenneriana*, a cross between yellow and least water-lilies. This is a national rarity, as it occurs in only about 15 localities in Britain. It is also found in St Germains and Dougalston lochs.

There are areas of wet woodland, with alder carr in seasonally flooded areas. The woodland includes some ornamental maples and cypress trees, as well as various native species. There used to be large areas of rhododendron, but some of these have been cleared.

The loch is rich in freshwater life. The Microscopical Society of Glasgow visited on several occasions in the 1890s to collect micro-organisms to study, and it remains a good place to go pond-dipping today. However, it is the larger animals and plants that are more likely to be seen by visitors. Perch and roach are regularly caught by fishermen. Common frogs are plentiful and often fall prey to grey herons. Mute swans,

Hybrid water-lilies and yellow flag-irises, Kilmardinny Loch.

© Richard Sutcliffe

© Richard Sutcliffe

Flower of hybrid water-lily.

© David Palmar (www.photoscot.co.uk)

Water rail.

mallard, coots and moorhens breed here, encouraged by regular feeding by visitors. It is not unusual to see great crested grebes and little grebes. Other rarities turn up sporadically.

In the summer months, Daubenton's bats catch insects from the surface of the loch at night, while grey squirrels and red foxes are seen in the area throughout the year.

Highlights

There are water rails at this site. Whilst not a very uncommon species, because of its secretive nature it is more likely to be heard than seen, but here you may be lucky enough to catch a glimpse of one amongst the trees at the water's edge on the southern shore of the loch. Both the male and the female water rail have chestnut-brown and black upperparts, grey face and underparts, black-and-white barred flanks, and a long red bill. It is smaller and slimmer than a moorhen. Water rails feed on small fish, snails and insects.

Activities

There are occasional events led by East Dunbartonshire and Mugdock Country Park Countryside Rangers. For details contact the Ranger Service (tel. 0141 956 6586) or see 'What's On' at www.mugdock-country-park.org.uk.

Also nearby

Tannoch Loch (NS 555 752) in Milngavie is about 2km to the north. It is a shallow man-made loch, which attracts mallard, tufted ducks, coots, moorhens and grey herons. Mute swans breed here and kingfishers are sometimes seen.
Dougalston Loch SINC (NS 562 737), where the hybrid water-lily can also be seen, and which is also a good site for common toads, is about 1.5km to the north-east.

Facilities

A wheelchair-friendly path runs around the loch.

How to get there

By train: Glasgow Central low level or Glasgow Queen Street low level to Hillfoot (Milngavie line). Exit the station on to Milngavie Rd, and turn right. Take the third road on the left (Kilmardinny Ave). Follow the road for a few hundred metres until you reach a footpath leading to the right into the site.

By bus: First bus 109 and 119 run along Milngavie Rd. Alight at the bus stop at the end of Kilmardinny Ave.

By car: Take the A81 from Glasgow. After passing Hillfoot Station turn left up Manse Rd, right into Kilmardinny Ave, then second left into Thomson Drive. There is a small area to park beside the loch at the end of this road.

Maps: Glasgow street map; OS Landranger 64, Explorer 342.

Ballagan Glen

A hidden wildlife and geological gem on the edge of the Campsie Fells

Grid refs: Entrance to main drive NS 572 794; the waterfall NS 573 799

This site is a deeply incised glen on the southern edge of the Campsie Fells, formerly used for overwintering sheep. Much of Ballagan Glen remains wooded because its steep sides have precluded heavy sheep grazing, unlike much of the high fell ground in the Campsies. The Spout of Ballagan waterfall cascades in a 20m sheer drop over the rock strata at the end of the glen, and to the south-west of the waterfall is the Ballagan Formation rock exposure. The site is managed by the Scottish Wildlife Trust, who own most of the land, and is designated as a Site of Special Scientific Interest.

The primary habitat is the relatively undisturbed and ancient gorge ash woodland. As well as ash, there is wych elm, bird cherry, gean, birch, alder, oak and rowan. Upland mixed ashwood is rare in this part of Scotland and there are a number of significant bryophytes (mosses and liverworts) that can be found in the relatively less accessible parts of the glen.

There are also areas of tall rank neutral grassland with smaller flushes – wet areas – along seepage lines within the rock strata. The flushes contain sedges and a more diverse assemblage of plants including orchids and in some places common butterwort.

Above the waterfall the vegetation is influenced more by rainfall than by the underlying strata, and is predominantly a mix of acidic heath and grassland with some base rich flush areas.

Dippers, grey wagtails, grey herons, tits, robins and thrushes occur within the reserve, and summer visitors include willow warblers and cuckoos. You may get good views of ravens, buzzards,

Part of the large exposure of the Ballagan Formation beside the waterfall.

© David Garner

The thickly wooded gorge of Ballagan Glen.

© David Garner

kestrels, sparrowhawks and even occasional peregrines. Rotting trees, leaf litter and shallow streamside pools all provide vital habitats, which support a number of uncommon beetles, flies and snails.

Highlights
The glen is the geological type locality for the Ballagan Formation (where it was first described), which is of Lower Carboniferous age: successive layers of distinctly coloured shales and cementstones are exposed on the western side of the glen, and can be clearly seen as you climb the path up the eastern side. These rocks were laid down in coastal lagoons about 350 million years ago. The water was very salty due to evaporation in the hot, tropical climate. Minerals such as gypsum are common here. Above these is a succession of basalt lava flows. The occasional Merlin may be seen in good weather hunting across the moor above the Spout. This area is also good for ferns with the locally rare adder's tongue fern and beech fern hidden away in the grassland.

Activities
There are occasional walks led by the Scottish Wildlife Trust and also East Dunbartonshire and Mugdock Country Park Countryside Rangers – for more details contact the SWT or Ranger Service (pp. 168 and 169) or look on www.clydeswt.org or www.mugdock-country-park.org.uk.

Also nearby
Fin Glen (NS 583 813), about 2km to the north-east, is a similar deeply incised glen with remnants of flora from before sheep grazing.

Note: The area around the waterfall should be avoided during wet weather as it is dangerous and there is considerable risk of slipping on wet ground or loose rocks. Stout footwear should be worn at all times. It is recommended that any visitors to the site keep to the main eastern path wherever possible.

Facilities
There is an information board at the entrance to the reserve.

How to get there
On foot: From the Kirkhouse Inn, Strathblane, walk eastwards along the A891 (Campsie Rd) past Strathblane Parish Church, and continue for about 1km. Take care: there is no footpath and the verge is narrow. Turn left into the main drive to Ballagan House (marked 'Private'). Immediately bear right, but at Ballagan House keep to the left of the house and go behind it. Past the garages, by a stile, is a sign pointing right to the reserve. Over the stile follow the path up through the woods until you reach a gate leading to open hillside. Bear left up the hillside and a fence marking the eastern boundary of the reserve will come into view. Aim for a stile where there is an information board.

By train and bus: Glasgow Central low level or Glasgow Queen Street low level to Milngavie. Exit the station, then take First bus 10 to Strathblane, and follow the directions given in the 'On foot' details above.

By bus: First bus 10 to Strathblane, and get off at the Kirkhouse Inn – follow the directions given in the 'On foot' details above.

By car: Please note: cars should not be parked at Ballagan House – vehicles should be left in public parking spaces at the nearby village of Strathblane. From there, follow the directions in the 'On foot' details above.

Maps: OS Landranger 64, Explorer 348; British Geological Survey S30E Glasgow; a reserve map can be downloaded from www.clydeswt.org.

Loch Ardinning

A loch with scarce aquatic plants and associated woodland, grassland and muir

Grid ref: Main entrance NS 563 779

Loch Ardinning Wildlife Reserve is a visitor-friendly haven with 142 hectares of varied upland habitat. The loch is of natural origin, occupying a glacially excavated hollow, but enlarged by a dam built across its north-western outflow in 1796. The reserve also includes an area of moorland, Muirhouse Muir, to the east of the loch, a lochan and some grassland and woodland. This diverse habitat in turn supports a great variety of wildlife. There are a number of scenic walks offering splendid views down the Blane Valley to Dumgoyne, Ben Lomond and the hills beyond Loch Lomond. The site has been a wildlife reserve since 1988, when the land was given to the Scottish Wildlife Trust.

To the north and east of the loch, including Muirhouse Muir, the peaty soils provide ideal conditions for acid-loving plants such as bog-myrtle, cranberry, crowberry, cowberry, bog asphodel, marsh violet and heath spotted-orchid, and there is a fine display of heather in late summer. The wet woodland and grassland west and south-west of the loch are fed by water issuing through basalt rock. This allows for plants that like a more neutral or alkaline environment, such as lady's bedstraw, common spotted-orchid, northern marsh-orchid and greater butterfly orchid.

At least 18 species of mammals and 113 species of birds have been recorded on the reserve. The loch itself attracts a variety of waterbirds. Grey herons are regular visitors and common breeding species include mallard, tufted duck, greylag goose, coot and little grebe. Outside the breeding season the most regular ducks are mallard, tufted duck, goldeneye and goosander, with occasional teal and wigeon.

The narrow north-west arm of the loch contains a reedbed from which water rails can often be heard at any time of year, with the occasional sedge warbler during the breeding season, in late spring and summer. Willow warblers breed in profusion along the north side of the loch, and this is also a good area to encounter reed buntings and tree pipits.

On Muirhouse Muir, skylarks, grasshopper warblers, stonechats and whinchats breed in small numbers. Curlews have also bred here. Red and black grouse can be seen at any time of year, whilst a few cuckoos make themselves known from early May onwards. Several species of birds of prey occur, including kestrel, buzzard, sparrowhawk, peregrine and hen harrier. Other birds of interest include lesser redpoll, bullfinch, crossbill, jay, raven, woodcock and great spotted and green woodpeckers.

The most common mammals are roe deer, rabbits, voles and wood mice. Less frequently seen are brown hare, red fox, stoat, weasel and otter. Moles advertise their presence with their hills in many parts of the reserve.

Water lobelia in flower.

© David C Shenton

© David C Shenton

Muirhouse Muir.

Common lizard, palmate newt, common frog and common toad are regularly recorded at Loch Ardinning. Large pike are the main goal for fishermen, and young pike can sometimes be seen in the shallow water by the dam. Perch are also present and eels are a favourite food for visiting grey herons.

At least 17 species of butterflies have been recorded, the most notable breeding species being green hairstreak, small pearl-bordered fritillary, small copper and orange-tip. Five species of dragonfly and five species of damselfly are resident. Beetles include the glow worm and violet oil beetles and large species of diving beetle.

The area to the west and south-west of the loch lies on basalt of the Clyde Plateau Volcanic Formation (see p. 17). This can be seen by the south-west corner of the loch, contrasting with younger sandstones and conglomerate exposed north and east of the loch. A quartz–dolerite dyke, about 5m wide by up to 2m high, runs west–east across the fields approximately 370m south of the loch.

Highlights
The loch contains a variety of aquatic plants, the most notable being water lobelia; its attractive flowers are spread over much of the loch in summer. Other water plants include bogbean, water plantain, marsh cinquefoil and the uncommon lesser marshwort.

Activities
There is an annual open day, occasional guided walks and volunteer days are held at least once a month – see www.clydeswt.org. Fishing is permitted, but for the sake of the birdlife please avoid the west side of the loch.

Note: On Muirhouse Muir dogs should be kept on a lead during the bird breeding season (April to August).

Facilities
There is a nature trail and a series of paths; the nature trail north of the loch is suitable for wheelchairs and can be accessed from the A81 lay-by and over the dam. More details can be found at www.clydeswt.org.

How to get there
On foot: There are pedestrian access points from the main lay-by and over the dam, and also at the southern end of the reserve.

By bus: First bus 10 runs along the A81 past the reserve and can drop off/pick up at the dam.

By car: From Glasgow take the A81 (Aberfoyle road). The reserve is about 4km north of Milngavie. The main parking spot is a lay-by on the east side of the A81, about 100m south of the dam. There are smaller lay-bys at the dam itself.

Maps: OS Landranger 64, Explorer 348; a reserve map can be downloaded from www.clydeswt.org.

North and east

North and east of Glasgow there is one of the largest and most intact lowland raised bogs in the UK, which is home to adders, lizards and carnivorous plants; there is also some spectacular geology, including somewhere to hunt for fossils, a former plantation that has gone wild, and even a chance to walk in the tree tops.

Campsie Glen

A wooded gorge which reveals the lava flows that formed the Campsie Fells

Grid refs: Clachan of Campsie car parking area NS 610 796; car park north of the glen NS 612 800

Campsie Glen is an attractive wooded glen that cuts into the south face of the Campsie Fells above the village of Clachan of Campsie. The Kirk Burn descends through the glen via a series of waterfalls. Both sedimentary rocks and lavas from the Carboniferous Period (359–299 million years ago) can be seen, and tell of a past that included tropical lagoons and volcanic eruptions. Campsie Glen is a Local Nature Conservation Site and a Regionally Important Geological Site.

Walking up the lower part of the glen, the first rock exposures you see in the bed and banks of the Kirk Burn are sedimentary rocks. These consist of layers of soft, grey mudstone with frequent, thin (10–30cm thick) beds of cream-coloured cementstone from the Ballagan Formation (see pp. 16 and 100), which were laid down in salty shallow waters in the hot climate of the Carboniferous, around 350 million years ago. The cementstone is harder and,

because it is more resistant to water erosion, tends to form small waterfalls. Slightly further upstream a larger waterfall, about 2m high, marks the point where a dyke of dolerite rock crosses the burn.

Further on the glen narrows, and the first of the lava flows can be seen in the cliffs. These lavas lie on top of the Ballagan Formation and are younger, at around 340 million years old. Known as the Clyde Plateau Volcanic Formation (see p. 17), they are mostly black, fine-grained basalt and form a lava pile over 500m thick. Typically, each individual flow has a hard solid centre with a softer, more friable top and base. Sometimes between flows there is a thin layer of soft material called red bole. This represents a 'fossil' soil that formed on the top of the lava flows before the next one was erupted. The upper, more open part of the glen cuts through further lava flows.

Campsie Glen contains semi-natural

Campsie Glen and the south slopes of the Campsie Fells.

Campsie Glen woods.

Waterfall over one of the Campsie Glen lava flows.

woodland, which recent planting has helped restore and extend. Trees include ash, oak, beech, sycamore, alder, birch and rowan. The damp, shady conditions in the lower glen are favourable for ferns and mosses, but there are also many flowering plants. The glen supports a rich variety of birds and other wildlife. Some of the trees provide potential roost sites for bats, and dead trees provide excellent habitat for fungi and invertebrates. Otters are known to frequent the area.

Highlights
A pleasant walk up this attractive glen provides an excellent opportunity to look at the basalt lavas that form the Campsie Fells.

Activities
There are occasional natural history walks and activities led by East Dunbartonshire and Mugdock Country Park Countryside Rangers – for details contact them (tel. 0141 956 6586) or see the 'What's On' section at www. mugdock-country-park.org.uk.

Also nearby
Sculliongour limestone quarry SSSI (NS 634 790) is so designated on account of the range of lime-loving flowers and mosses that grow there. Fossils can be found in the spoil heaps.

Corrie Burn SSSI, above the village of Queenzieburn (NS 695 774). In this area, a number of streams expose a section through Carboniferous limestones, shales and other rocks, some of which are very rich in fossils.

Note: Unstable and slippery rocks make it unwise to continue up the glen past the warning notice – the upper part of the glen is better accessed separately, as described below.

How to get there

On foot: The lower part of the glen is accessed from Clachan of Campsie, from behind the building at the car parking area. From here the upper, more open, part of the glen can also be reached on foot: take the signposted steep path up the side of the glen to the car park on the B822, and from there follow the path down into the upper glen.

By bus: First bus X85 to Clachan of Campsie. The car park on the B822 above Lennoxtown is not served by a scheduled bus, but the on-demand MyBus Rural 600 service covers this area (tel. 0845 128 4037).

By car: Leave Glasgow by the A803 (Springburn Rd) through Bishopbriggs and take the A807 to Torrance, turning right here on to the B822 to Lennoxtown. For the lower part of the glen, turn left and go through the town on the A891 (towards Strathblane) until the turn-off for Clachan of Campsie. There is a car park in the village. For the upper part of the glen, take the B822 (Fintry road) north of Lennoxtown to the car park.

Maps: OS Landranger 64, Explorer 348; British Geological Survey S030E Glasgow and S031W Airdrie.

Blairskaith Quarry

A great place to find fossils – of creatures that lived about 330 million years ago

Grid ref: Quarry entrance NS 595 752

Blairskaith Quarry is set into the south-facing slopes of Blairskaith Muir between Torrance and Milngavie. A brick-clay pit abandoned since the late 1970s, it is significant for both its abundant extinct fossils and habitats supporting a variety of plant and animal life, with large shallow pools of water that last throughout the year and some well-drained lime-rich soils. The quarry is a Local Nature Conservation Site.

The rocks of Blairskaith Quarry date from the upper part of the Lower Limestone Formation of Carboniferous age (about 330 million years ago). They represent around 100,000 years in the history of the Earth: the sediments that would later form rocks were slowly laid down as the environment oscillated between marine and non-marine.

Blairskaith Quarry looking south.
1: Campsie Clayband Ironstones; 2: Blackhall Limestone.

Solitary corals.

The site was probably on the margins of a large delta further to the east, with large bays and lagoons being alternately open to the sea or river-dominated.

The oldest rocks at the site, which are exposed on the base of the quarry, are shales and sideritic (iron carbonate) ironstones known as the Campsie Clayband Ironstones. These are mainly non-marine deposits,

but gradually become more marine near the top. The upper part of this sequence contains sun-cracked horizons and a thin bone-bed, indicating that this area was above water at this time.

Sketch map of the quarry showing the location of rock types. The key shows the geological sequence.

Neilson Shell Bed

Blackhall Limestone

Campsie Clayband Ironstones

Exposure outline

Road/path

Quarry perimeter

Small paths

Gastropods.

Orthocones.

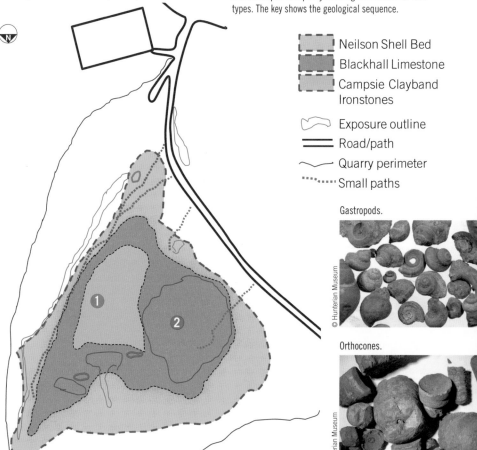

109

Above these is the Blackhall Limestone, the main limestone here, which forms a prominent sloping platform in the centre of the quarry. It is about 1m thick, and in two distinct sections. The lower part is a band with two thin limestones containing ostracods – minute shelled organisms. The upper part is a thicker, muddier crinoidal limestone that contains many fossils – especially crinoids (sea animals that look as if they have stems and arms, commonly called 'sea lilies'), together with goniatites and orthocones (fore-runners of ammonites with chambered shells), brachiopods (also known as lamp shells – marine animals with two shells), gastropods (snail-like molluscs) and solitary corals. Rare trilobites (extinct marine arthropods) are occasionally found.

At the top of the exposed sequence, around the edge of the quarry, is the Neilson Shell Bed, which consists of a series of rusty black shales, some of which

© Hunterian Museum

Trilobite.

show marine influence and contain many fossils – especially molluscs. In between these fossil-rich shales, there are layers without fossils, suggesting the input of river mud. Concretions of hard cemented shale formed within the softer shales have yielded remains of the river fish *Watsonichthys*. Towards the lip of the quarry, layers rich in ostracods of a type found in shallow brackish to marine waters may be collected.

Crinoid stems.

Blackhall Limestone with crinoids.

© Hunterian Museum

© Hunterian Museum

Juniper haircap moss.

Downy birch, goat willow and alder have colonized a considerable part of the quarry and ferns, horsetails and mosses grow well in the damper parts. There is a rich variety of flowering plants, which provide nectar for insects, including butterflies and hoverflies. The insects are food for many birds and you may be lucky enough to see a green woodpecker feeding on ants within the quarry.

Brown hares sometimes venture into the quarry from neighbouring fields. Areas of standing water support palmate newts and common frogs and great crested newts have been seen nearby in the past.

Highlights

Large areas of the quarry are left exposed to weathering and erosion, which allows quite exquisite and complete fossils to be collected loose from the gentle slopes. There are literally hundreds of fossils in every square metre of exposed Blackhall Limestone. The site is important for the evidence of ancient marine biodiversity it provides, and for the different groups of fossils, which reflect how, throughout the sequence, the environment frequently changed from marine to freshwater and back again.

Also nearby

Sculliongour limestone quarry SSSI (NS 634 790). This is cut into marine limestones of a similar age to the limestone at Blairskaith – the quarry does not have the same abundance of fossils, but is important because it shows how the environment changed over short distances.

Campsie Glen (p. 106) and **Ballagan Glen** (p. 100), further west from Lennoxtown, have non-marine deposits, which are also largely unfossiliferous but of interest

because they provide us with a record of past changes in the environment – before the sediments at Blairskaith were deposited, the area was characterized first by warm lagoons and then by volcanic eruptions.

How to get there

By bus: A number of buses stop at Balmore, 2.5km away from the quarry: Henderson Travel 68 (from Glasgow) and 47/47A (Monklands Hospital–Milngavie, via Cumbernauld). From the bus stop at Balmore, walk uphill: along Glenorchard Rd for 2km, then at Mealybrae House turn left on to Tower Rd to Easter Blairskaith Farm and go up the road past the farm to the quarry. Alternatively, phone 0845 128 4037 in advance to book the MyBus Rural 600 service to take you onwards from Balmore.

By car: From Glasgow, follow the A803 out of Glasgow through Bishopbriggs, or the A879 towards Milngavie, then the A807 to Balmore. Turn north up the Glenorchard Rd and then left on Tower Rd until Easter Blairskaith Farm. There is space for a car to park responsibly without blocking farm access to East Blairskaith – please ask at the house for permission.

Maps: Glasgow street map; OS Landranger 64, Explorer 342; British Geological Survey S30E Glasgow.

Cadder Wilderness

A former plantation with stately beech trees, varied fungi and rare insects

Grid ref: Entrance from the Forth & Clyde Canal towpath NS 600 714

Cadder Wilderness is a dense semi-natural woodland, 40 hectares in size, which lies on a low hill just north of the Forth & Clyde Canal near Bishopbriggs. The land would once have been much wetter, but extensive drainage works and tree planting has greatly changed its character. The woodland began as a plantation in the 1740s. The trees were laid out to represent the battle formation of British troops and their French opponents at the Battle of Dettingen of 1743 – they were designed to be a lasting celebration of British victory. The woodland became progressively wilder over time, making it a magnet for naturalists in the nineteenth century, particularly eminent local entomologists: the rare and interesting insects they found were key to the wood's designation as a Site of Special Scientific Interest.

The wilderness is situated on top of sedimentary rocks of the Carboniferous Upper Limestone Formation. These rocks include several seams of coal and ironstone, which have been mined extensively in the area. Coal was mined here until the 1930s, and the remains of one coal pit, the associated buildings and spoil heap are still evident in the south-west corner of the site.

The woodland comprises a mixture of living and dead trees, of various species and including a range of states of decay, making it ideal for fungi: the fruiting bodies are at their most spectacular in autumn. Look on dead beechwood for clusters of porcelain fungus, with translucent caps, or the boldly striped many-zoned polypore bracket fungus. The canopy is characterized by birch and oak with rowan and beech, the latter often marking old drains and local groves. The ground flora reflects the acidic nature of the soil: there are grasses, wood sorrel, broad buckler fern and mosses, and remnants of heathland and marsh. In the late spring and summer you may spot the attractive blooms of the common spotted-orchid and broad-leaved helleborine along the paths.

Most of the notable insects found at Cadder require dead and decaying wood to survive, including nationally scarce flies and beetles. Among these are: a fly whose young need oak, *Aulacigaster leucopeza*; a hoverfly which is attracted to sap runs on birch, *Brachyopa insensilis*; and a bronzy-black predatory ground beetle that is typically found under rotting tree bark, *Pterostichus oblongatus*.

Cadder Wilderness, with dead wood in the foreground.

Broad-leaved helleborine.

There are also larger animals of interest. Roe deer inhabit these woods, and buzzards often perch on the dead trees alongside the wilderness's southern path. Sparrowhawks, great spotted woodpeckers and willow tits are resident all year round. Redstarts and wood and garden warblers may be spotted between April and September, and redwings pay winter visits.

Highlights

The beech tree is not native to Scotland but it is key to several species at the site. There are some impressive and aged beeches dotted around the margin of the wood, which are believed to be the remnants of the eighteenth-century plantation.

A sawfly has been named after Cadder Wilderness, where it was first discovered: *Nematus cadderensis*. *Nematus* sawflies are particularly diverse in northern woodlands, where they rely on living plants.

The sawfly *Nematus cadderensis*, named after this site.

How to get there

On foot or by bicycle: The site can be accessed from the Forth & Clyde Canal towpath.

By train: Glasgow Queen Street to Bishopbriggs (Edinburgh via Falkirk and Croy lines). From the station approach, head straight on along Kirkintilloch Rd. After 500m turn left and follow Balmuildy Rd for about 1km. Cross the bridge over the canal and turn immediately left on to the canal path. The entrance to the wilderness, which has no sign, is the first path on your right.

By bus: First buses 27 and 88 both stop at Balmuildy Rd. Alight here and follow the directions given from Balmuildy Rd in the 'By train' details.

By car: Take the A803 (Kirkintilloch road) from Port Dundas to Bishopbriggs. About 500m after the town centre, turn left into Balmuildy Rd: there is street parking off Balmuildy Rd, south of the canal. From here, walk across the bridge and follow the directions from the canal given in the 'By train' details.

Maps: Glasgow street map; OS Landranger 64, Explorer 342.

© Natural History Museum

Flanders Moss National Nature Reserve

One of the largest and most intact lowland raised bogs in the UK

Grid ref: Car park NS 647 978

Flanders Moss is a huge and fine example of scarce lowland raised bog habitat, which offers the visitor a glimpse of a wild and ancient landscape filled with rare and specialized wildlife. It formed on an estuary as the sea retreated down the Carse of Stirling after the last Ice Age, and it has been growing and depositing peat for 8000 years. The moss has suffered from human interference in the past, losing about 40 per cent of its area during peat clearances in the 1700s and 1800s, and more recently diminished because of conifer plantations and ditching for peat extraction. But now 95 per cent of the peat body is undergoing restoration work, and the site is being managed by Scottish Natural Heritage as a National Nature Reserve.

Common lizard. © David Pickett/SNH

As with all bog habitats, there is a limited but specialized range of plants, and these can be seen from the reserve's viewing tower and path. The surface vegetation looks spectacular from here, showing all the variation arising from different levels of wetness. When viewed up close, peatland plants such as round-leaved sundew and white beak-sedge can be seen to nestle amongst different types of sphagnum

mosses, giving a colourful mosaic of ground floras. In June the whole moss is covered with the white fluffy seed heads of two species of cottongrass.

In summer Flanders Moss is filled with birdsong. With luck, skylark, meadow pipit, redstart, willow warbler, tree pipit, stonechat and whinchat can all be heard from the boardwalk. It is one of the best places in the area to hear cuckoos and common snipe can be heard drumming – the sound made by males as part of their courtship display flights. The pools and ditches provide homes for dragonflies such as the common hawker and black and common darter, and several damselflies. On sunny days green tiger beetles prowl along the paths, and the rare large heath butterfly that breeds far out on the moss can be seen from the boardwalk.

In winter it is quieter but there is still a chance of seeing hen harrier, merlin and raven, while at dawn and dusk thousands of pink-footed and greylag geese head over the moss on their way to roost at the nearby Lake of Menteith. From the viewing tower at any time of the year, roe deer and red deer can both be seen feeding out on the moss.

Highlights

The boardwalk has been adopted by common lizards. They use it to bask

Round-leaved sundew.

© David Pickett/SNH

© David Pickett/SNH

The boardwalk at Flanders Moss.

on and on a good day anything up to 20 individuals can be seen by a visitor. Flanders Moss has a healthy population of adders and they have been seen close to the boardwalk.

Activities

A programme of events is being developed and details about these and further information about the bog can be found at www.nnr-scotland.org.uk. You can also contact the reserve manager by phoning the SNH Stirling office on 01786 450 362.

Green tiger beetle.

© David Pickett/SNH

Facilities

A 900m path and boardwalk enables people to safely visit the moss – both are suitable for wheelchairs – and a 7m viewing tower gives an impressive outlook. Walking off the path is not encouraged because of the number of hidden, deep water-filled ditches across the moss – finding one of these can really spoil your day!

How to get there

By bicycle: It is possible to cycle the 17km from Stirling; the route between the station and the reserve is fairly flat and longer diversions along quieter lanes can be made for part of it. There is a bicycle rack in the reserve's car park.

By train and bus: Glasgow Queen Street to Stirling, about 17km from Flanders Moss. First bus C11 from Stirling goes to Thornhill, about 2km from the reserve entrance along the B822.

By car: From the A811 (Drymen–Stirling road) turn north at the Kippen roundabout on to the B822, following the brown tourist signs. After 3km, turn left at the Flanders Moss NNR sign and follow the track to the end. From the A873 (Blairdrummond–Aberfoyle road), turn south in Thornhill village on to the B822, follow the brown tourist signs and after 2km turn right, down the access track at the Flanders Moss NNR sign. There is a car park at the end of the track.

Maps: OS Landranger 57, Explorer 366.

Lenzie Moss

A recovering lowland raised bog with insect-eating plants

Grid ref: Lenzie Station NS 654 719

This important area of peatland is a lowland raised bog that lies at the edge of Lenzie in East Dunbartonshire. It has a rich variety of wildlife habitats, including wet heath, birch woodland and untouched primary bog. Lenzie Moss is designated as a Local Nature Reserve and a Local Nature Conservation Site.

Formation of the bog probably started some 11,500 years ago, after the glaciers of the last Ice Age retreated and left behind a shallow loch, which over thousands of years was filled by plant material to create a domed raised bog. It is presumably on account of its former domed appearance that Lenzie Moss has also been called Mountain Moss, but the dome is now non-existent due to peat extraction.

Historical records of peat removal go back a long time. The Charter of Alexander II, dated 1226, allowed the canons of Cambuskenneth to dig peat from the site. During the late nineteenth century the Glasgow–Edinburgh railway was constructed, with the line running

Lenzie Moss.

through the middle of the moss: a large quantity of peat was removed. In the mid twentieth century, up until the 1960s, the Lenzie Peat Development Company extracted peat commercially for horticultural use. The company was responsible for trench digging and breaching the moss with a narrow-gauge railway line, which went to Lenzie train station.

The scars of peat extraction can be seen across the centre of the site, but many of the 'peat fields', with baulks and hollows, are starting to recover. Active management including the blocking of drainage channels and the felling of invasive birch is being carried out to help with the restoration process. Perhaps one day the moss may even have a dome again.

The birch woodland bordering the railway is dominated by downy birch but also contains holly, hazel and rowan – a rich native woodland mix. It supports woodland moths such as the silvery arches and the striking large emerald. Long-tailed tits and treecreepers can be seen searching the trees for food, whilst the woodland floor includes bilberries, with dark-blue berries in the autumn.

On the raised bog there are plants that thrive on the nutrient-poor peat. During the summer fluffy hare's-tail cottongrass carpets the bog in white and bog asphodel provides patches of gold. The tiny round-leaved sundew has a clever way of enhancing its diet. Its hairy leaves secrete a sticky liquid, and any small insect that lands of a leaf will be trapped. Over time the leaf closes and the plant digests the fleshy parts of the insect.

During the summer the wet boggy areas are full of insect life. The common hawker and black darter dragonflies roam the moss looking for prey, and brightly coloured large red and common blue damselflies can be seen dancing over the boggy pools.

© Mugdock Country Park

Above: Male common blue damselfly.

Left: Bog-rosemary.

Highlights

The nationally scarce bog-rosemary occurs on the bog at Lenzie Moss, the only site in East Dunbartonshire to have this tiny evergreen plant. It has pale pink flowers in May and June and is one of the few peatland species that occurs exclusively on lowland raised bogs.

Activities

Public events and a conservation volunteer group are led by the Friends of Lenzie Moss and by the East Dunbartonshire and Mugdock Country Park Ranger Service. Details can be obtained from the Ranger Service tel. 0141 956 6586 and from the websites www.mugdock-country-park.org and www.friendsoflenziemoss.org.uk.

Also nearby

The Gadloch (NS 644 708) on the outskirts of Lenzie, just south of the moss, supports a large bird population, particularly during winter months, including greylag geese and whooper swans.

Facilities

A 2.3km wheelchair-accessible path circuits the moss.

How to get there

By train: Glasgow Queen Street to Lenzie (Croy line). The entrance to the moss is at the far end of the station car park, on the north side of the line.

By bus: First bus X85: alight at Auchinloch Rd opposite Millersneuk Rd. It is a two-minute walk in a northerly direction to Lenzie Station, from where you can enter the moss at the end of the car park.

By car: From Glasgow drive east on the M8 and join the M80, then take the B757, which is signposted to Kirkintilloch. Drive through Auchinloch to Lenzie Station: the entrance to the moss is at the end of the car park. Further parking and access to the moss is available at Hawthorn Ave, three streets to the north of the station. The moss can also be accessed on its western side from Heather Drive (NS 644 719), off Boghead Rd.

Maps: Glasgow street map; OS Landranger 64, Explorer 342.

117

Bar Hill

The site of a Roman fort with woodland plants, animals and fungi

Grid ref: War memorial, Main St, Twechar NS 701 757

The long mound of Bar Hill rises sharply out of the floodplain of the Kelvin Valley on the north-east outskirts of Glasgow. At the top there are spectacular panoramic views and Bar Hill Roman fort, one of the best-known sites along the line of the Antonine Wall. A variety of wildlife habitats make up a rich patchwork of biodiversity, including broadleaved woodland, conifer plantation, acid grassland and pockets of marsh. Bar Hill is designated as a Local Nature Conservation Site.

The broadleaved woodlands to the south of the Roman fort are dominated by mature sycamore and beech, which when wandered through give a cathedral-like feel to the woodland. Other species such as ash, rowan, birch and pedunculate oak make up a good native woodland mix. The woodland floor has a rich variety of plants including the shade-loving broad buckler fern, lady-fern, wood-sedge and wood horsetail. Bluebells carpet the woodland in late spring, whilst in the summer heath bedstraw and wood sage flourish.

To the east of the Roman fort, heather and bilberry can be found on the floor of

Honey fungus.

the conifer plantations of spruce, Scots pine and larch. Green woodpecker, tawny owl, roe deer and badger inhabit the woods.

The site supports areas of acid grassland, and there species such as heath spotted-orchid, pill sedge and devil's-bit scabious make a colourful sight in the summer months. Green hairstreak butterflies can be spotted in May and June.

In the autumn visitors can see many species of fungi, including porcelain fungus, fly agaric, honey fungus, common yellow russula and hoof fungus. The borders of the amenity grassland at the Roman fort support the tiny parrot waxcap – a lovely green and yellow waxy mushroom with a peaked cap.

Fly agarics.

Hoof fungus.

© Mugdock Country Park

Highlights

Bar Hill in winter.

Bar Hill has a fascinating geological past. The high ground is formed from an outcrop of a sill – a flat sheet – of the igneous rock dolerite. It is part of the Midland Valley sill which dates from the end of the Carboniferous Period, around 300 million years ago. It is in the typical asymmetrical shape of a 'crag and tail': the crag is a steep slope on the west side and the tail a more gentle slope to the east. This shape was created by the passage of glacial ice, and indicates that the ice flowed in an easterly direction.

Also nearby

Dumbreck Marsh LNR (NS 703 775) on the outskirts of Kilsyth supports a large bird population, including water rails. The reserve is a good place for both birdwatching and nature walks.

How to get there

By bus: First bus 27/27B runs to Twechar. There is a bus stop on Glen Shirva Rd. From there, walk up Main St to reach the war memorial and the start of the track to Bar Hill.

By car: Head north on the A803 from Glasgow. After Kirkintilloch and take the first road on the right signposted for Twechar (B8023). Turn right over the Forth & Clyde Canal into Twechar and park opposite the war memorial at the Barhill Lane Industrial Site. Bar Hill is signposted from the war memorial.

Maps: Glasgow street map; OS Landranger 64, Explorer 348.

Luggiebank Wood

Quiet woodland and riverside walks just south of Cumbernauld

Grid refs: Reserve entrances NS 758 731 and NS 755 729

Luggiebank Wood comprises almost 30 hectares of woodland and grassland along the banks of the Luggie Water. It is just to the south of Cumbernauld, but has a secluded atmosphere away from the hustle and bustle of the town centre. The woodland has a rich array of wildflowers, particularly in the spring, and in places the meandering river passes through shallow pools. The grassland area is good for butterflies and orchids. The site is a Scottish Wildlife Trust reserve and a Site of Importance for Nature Conservation.

Alders, which occur in the reserve, with green cones that turn black when ripe.

© Jackie Gilliland

The woodland areas contain flora typical of long-established woodland sites, with oak and birch, bluebell, primrose, greater stichwort and opposite-leaved golden-saxifrage. The grassland beside the river contains a few local rarities including melancholy thistle, pale sedge and greater butterfly orchid, a species which is declining in the area due to agricultural improvement and woodland planting.

The path through Luggiebank Wood.

© Scottish Wildlife Trust

Wych elm and ash are present alongside the Luggie Water, where alkaline soil conditions prevail, and in flushes – wet areas – along the southern slopes of the site. Previously, much of the reserve's wych elm was devastated by Dutch elm disease and subsequently removed. The gaps left have been exploited by saplings of ash and sycamore. One area has been widely planted with sycamore in the past. Here dog's mercury, lesser celandine and water avens are the major components of the ground flora.

The woodland is quite open with a high abundance of grasses in the ground flora. Broad buckler fern is common, with hard fern, and great wood-rush is also present. Greater stichwort and red campion occur in significant patches with some primrose and common dog-violet.

The grassland is typically rich in broadleaved herbs – ribwort plantain, common knapweed, common sorrel and lesser stichwort – but where the surface is flushed with surface streams the variety of plants becomes greater. These areas include dominant tall herbs, such as meadowsweet and common valerian, but

Kingfisher with fish prey.

© Glasgow City Council

Highlights

A breeding population of kingfishers feed on the fish in the Luggie Water, which include brown trout.

Activities

Occasional activities are organized at the reserve by the Scottish Wildlife Trust, including practical conservation work. For further information see the SWT's Clyde Branch Member Centre at www.clydeswt.org.

Also nearby

Cumbernauld Glen Reserve (NS 777 763), also SWT managed, is about 3km north of Luggiebank.

also considerable numbers of common spotted-orchid and rarer plants such as greater butterfly orchid and goatsbeard.

Grey wagtail and dipper are among the birds regularly seen along the river. Long-eared owl, grasshopper warbler, wood warbler and lesser whitethroat have bred here.

Pipistrelle and Daubenton's bats can be seen at night feeding over the Luggie Water, although no signs of roosting have as yet been found. The two most important mammals are badgers and otters. Roe deer and red fox regularly pass through the site as it forms a wildlife corridor around the southern edge of Cumbernauld.

There is a good invertebrate fauna, including spiders typical of long-established woodland and nine species of butterfly, including the locally rare small pearl-bordered fritillary.

Carboniferous rocks of the Upper Limestone Formation, which are about 320 million years old, underlie the Luggiebank area. Some are exposed at the Lenziemill end of the reserve. Limestone outcrops at the very eastern edge, and shales and sandstones are exposed on either side of the Luggie Water.

Note: The footpath is located very close to the edge of the Luggie Water and drainage ditches. Horse riding takes place on the reserve.

How to get there

By train: Glasgow Queen Street to Greenfaulds (Cumbernauld line). Walk through the station's car park and cross over Lenziemill Rd. The reserve is accessible through a metal kissing gate and the footpath will lead you to the Luggie Water.

By car: From Glasgow take the M80, then the A80 (at a stretch which at the time of writing is being upgraded to motorway). Take the A8011 for Cumbernauld town centre, then follow the B8039 (signposted Park and Ride). At the double roundabout, turn right at the first roundabout and then go straight on from the second to Lenziemill Rd heading east (signposted A73). Drive past the SWT entrance sign to your left and park in the large car park at Greenfaulds Station, which is further along on the right.

Maps: Glasgow street map; OS Landranger 64; Explorer 349.

Palacerigg Country Park

A specially created country park with an emphasis on conservation and rare breeds

Grid ref: Main entrance NS 784 730

Set in the hills to the south-east of Cumbernauld, Palacerigg Country Park was established in the early 1970s, from what had been a bleak upland farm to the east of the then 'new town'. It comprises 300 hectares of grassland, moorland, woodland and ponds, which provide breeding sites and places of refuge for a large variety of wildlife. Hundreds of thousands of native trees and shrubs have been planted. Palacerigg has been developed around the objectives of conservation, environmental education and countryside recreation.

The country park has a rare breeds collection, which includes various ponies, sheep, cattle, goats, pigs and poultry. There are also red deer, and a children's farm with many tame domestic animals.

The wilder areas of the park have good populations of roe deer, badgers and red foxes, as well as buzzards, sparrowhawks, kestrels and long-eared owls. Brown hares and short-eared owls are sometimes seen. Glencryan Meadow, Fannyside Moor, Toddle Moor and Herd Hill are all good places for insects. Green hairstreak and small pearl-bordered fritillary butterflies

Toddle Moor, Palacerigg.

can be found here.

The moorland contains large areas of heather, which are a mass of purple in August, and occasional heath spotted-orchids can be found. The heather supports northern eggar moths – the males can be seen patrolling the area in early spring, searching for females. Meadow pipits nest in the heather, and short-eared owls search for bank voles.

On the edges of some of the fairways of the adjoining Palacerigg Golf Club, and elsewhere, large patches of pink and violet cuckoo flower in spring provide nectar and also food for caterpillars of both the green-veined white and orange-tip butterflies. Other wildflowers swathe some of the grassland in summer, among them tormentil, cat's ear and heath bedstraw.

Highlights

The only Scottish flock of bean geese (winter visitors from Sweden) often roost at night at the eastern side of the country park on the Fannyside Lochs and are sometimes seen feeding on Fannyside Moor during the day. Getting to where you would have a reasonable chance of seeing the geese involves a long walk across the moor without paths so boots are recommended.

The country park boasts a high-level wooden walkway, located near the start of the Laverock Trail, which allows visitors a bird's-eye view of the woodland area and the countryside around it, and to see trees and birds close up. You may get good sightings of birds such goldcrest, tits, warblers, finches, great spotted woodpecker and jay.

Activities

The visitor centre caters for both youngsters and adult groups, and has a thriving nature club. Throughout the year

the North Lanarkshire Countryside Ranger Service runs a programme of guided walks, activities and special events related to a wide range of environmental topics. For more details phone the Ranger Service on 01236 780 636 or look on www. northlanarkshire.gov.uk (see p. 168).

Also nearby
The Cumbernauld Greenspaces (Scottish Wildlife Trust), which consist of four nature reserves: Luggiebank (see p. 120); Forest Woods, on the southern edge of Cumbernauld, including Glencryan Wood; Northside Woods, a strip of woodland running alongside the A80, from Cumbernauld village to Ravenswood playing fields, and which acts as a wildlife corridor; and Cumbernauld Glen, a beautiful ancient woodland in the heart of Cumbernauld. For more information see www.clydeswt.org.

© David Palmar (www.photoscot.co.uk)

Bean geese.

Tree-top walkway.

Opening hours and facilities

The visitor centre, with displays, information panels and an exhibition area, is open April–Sept daily 9am–7pm and Oct–March daily 9am–4.15pm. There is a children's play area, gift shop, café, car parks, picnic sites and toilets, including wheelchair-accessible ones. The park includes 10km of bridle paths and a series of nature trails. The major paths in the central area are wheelchair-friendly. For more information phone 01236 720 047 or email palaceriggparkreception@northlan.gov.uk.

How to get there

By train: Glasgow Queen Street to Cumbernauld. The station is about 3km from the park and there is no public transport, but taxis are available.

By bus: First bus X5 to Cumbernauld College on Carbrain Rd. The journey to the park is about 3.5km and there is no public transport, but there are taxis.

By car: From Glasgow, take the M80, then A80 (at a stretch which at the time of writing is being upgraded to motorway). Then take the A8011 for Cumbernauld town centre and follow the brown signs for Palacerigg Country Park. There is a large car park.

Maps: Glasgow street map; OS Landranger 64 and Explorer 349.

West

To the west of Glasgow there is a sandy beach with rock pools on the shore of the Firth of Clyde, the mudflats of the Clyde Estuary with internationally important bird populations, upland sites which are home to hen harriers, and valuable habitats for dragonflies, water voles and otters. There is even a hidden gem right beside Glasgow Airport.

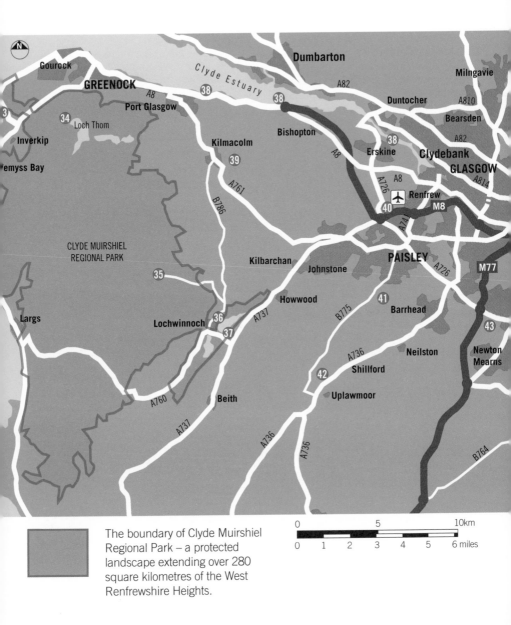

The boundary of Clyde Muirshiel Regional Park – a protected landscape extending over 280 square kilometres of the West Renfrewshire Heights.

Lunderston Bay

A sandy beach not far from Glasgow

Grid ref: Car park NS 204 746

Lunderston Bay is a popular beauty spot on the shore of the Firth of Clyde. It has a sandy beach and magnificent views across to Dunoon and the Cowal Peninsula and down towards Arran. There is a pleasant 1.5km shoreline walk to Ardgowan Point (NS 199 729). The site is part of Clyde Muirshiel Regional Park.

The rock pools exposed at low tide are alive with seashore animals including fish such as gobies, pipefish and shannies. Small shrimps, prawns and seaweeds such as bladderwrack and sea lettuce can be seen. The strand lines – of seaweed and other debris washed up on the beach – also provide cover and food for a variety of marine life. Sandhoppers hide here, and the empty egg cases of rays and dogfish, along with common jellyfish, are left behind by the tide. Under the beach, razor shells and lugworms feed when the tide is high before retiring into the sand as the water recedes.

As the beach becomes exposed at low tide there is the opportunity to watch wading birds such as common sandpiper and redshank catching small invertebrates. Eider ducks sometimes form large flocks offshore, of up to about 500 birds in summer, mainly moulting males. In spring a pair of shelduck can sometimes be seen feeding at low water, and wigeon are occasionally sighted in winter. Curlew and oystercatcher are present in the bay most of the year, with the largest numbers in winter, feeding on small crabs, shellfish and other invertebrates.

Lunderston Bay, looking across the Firth of Clyde.

© Clyde Muirshiel Regional Park

© Clyde Muirshiel Regional Park

A great variety of marine creatures are exposed at low tide.

Lunderston has a raised beach (see p. 19), with sandstone cliffs many metres back from the present shoreline. Ramsons grow over the ground at the base of these cliffs, and in the early spring the scent of garlic from the white flowers is heavy in the air. Next to the shoreline path there are marine plants such as thrift and sea radish, which have adapted to the salty conditions.

The mixed woodland area provides cover for roe deer who forage on the farmland areas at dawn and dusk.

Highlights

Low tide exposes rock pools containing seashore creatures including starfish, hermit crabs, beadlet anemone and butterfish. Common and Atlantic grey seals and harbour porpoises are often spotted offshore. Between spring and autumn, watch out for diving gannets, especially during July and August when they are often joined by feeding flocks of Manx shearwater.

Activities

Events at the beach include the Marine Conservation Society environmental initiatives Adopt a Beach and Beachwatch, and rock-pool dipping and shoreline walks. For more details contact the Clyde Muirshiel Regional Park Ranger Service (tel. 01505 614 791) or look on www.clydemuirshiel.co.uk.

Atlantic grey seal.

© David Palmar (www.photoscot.co.uk)

Facilities

Lunderston Bay has a car park with toilets, a picnic area and a children's play area. Sustrans National Cycle Route 75 follows the first part of the shoreline walk and is suitable for wheelchairs.

How to get there

By train: Glasgow Central to Inverkip (Wemyss Bay line). The station is 4km from the site, so taking a bicycle might make this journey easier: on exiting the station, head north on Station Ave, turn right on to Main St and right again on to the A78 (Inverkip Rd) – at the roundabout turn left along Cloch Rd for 1.5km.

By bus: McGill's 901 passes the entrance to the car park – on the coastal road A770 (Cloch Rd) opposite Cardwell Garden Centre and marked with a small brown sign saying 'picnic site'.

By car: From Glasgow take the M8/A78 through Greenock and before Inverkip turn on to the A770 and follow the brown signs. From Ayrshire take the A78 towards Greenock, after Inverkip turn on to the A770 and follow the brown signs.

Maps: OS Landranger 63, Explorer 341.

Greenock Cut

Moorland walks and a wooded glen

Grid ref: Visitor centre NS 246 721

The Greenock Cut Visitor Centre is situated at the heart of Inverclyde's water catchment area, near the Greenock and Kelly Cuts – narrow canal-like aqueducts that were constructed in the 1820s and 1840s to take water from Loch Thom to Greenock and from the Kelly Reservoir above Wemyss Bay to the Greenock Cut at Cornalees Bridge. Part of the Clyde Muirshiel Regional Park, the visitor centre is surrounded by moorland and is the starting point for several walks within the regional park. From nearby Dunrod Hill there are panoramic views across the Clyde Estuary. Shielhill Glen, also fairly close by, is a Site of Special Scientific Interest.

One of the walks follows the Greenock Cut towpath. Another, a circular nature trail, passes parts of the cuts and leads down into Shielhill Glen, following the Kip Water through mixed deciduous woodland and returning via unimproved pastureland. The Kelly Cut walk takes you through moorland along a towpath to Wemyss Bay.

The woodland species in Shielhill Glen include oak, ash and wych elm in the lower sections, with birch and rowan dominating further up. The rich ground flora includes pendulous sedge and great horsetail, with several species of orchid, including northern marsh-orchid and fragrant orchid, thriving in the moorland flushes (wet areas). The glen was partially carved out by the extraction of sandstone blocks between 1860 and about 1885 – for building in Greenock – and some can still be seen lying coated with moss.

There are several significant bird species in the area, including hen harrier, redstart (for which this is one of very few regular breeding sites in Inverclyde) and wood warbler. There is a remarkable inland breeding gull colony, with almost all of the Clyde area's breeding great black-backed gulls on the island in Loch Thom, as well as common gulls, herring gulls and lesser black-backed gulls. Some greylag and Canada geese also reside and breed in the area.

The Greenock Cut, looking to the Arrochar Alps.

© Clyde Muirshiel Regional Park

© Richard Sutcliffe

Golden-ringed dragonfly.

© Clyde Muirshiel Regional Park

Grass-of-Parnassus.

Highlights

The flora of the glen is particularly rich and includes species such as grass-of-Parnassus and bog asphodel in the wetter areas, as well as round-leaved sundew and common butterwort in the sphagnum moss and several fern species in the shadier parts. Woodland plants such as red campion and wood crane's-bill thrive in the dappled light, and ragged-robin is present in wet grassland areas. The Kelly Cut is a great place to see golden-ringed dragonfly and emerald damselfly as they hunt for insects over the water. On warm summer days the iridescent green tiger beetle can be seen along sandy stretches of the Kelly Cut footpath. The kingfisher is a frequent visitor. During the breeding season live images of swallows from a webcam can usually be seen in the visitor centre, showing the progress from eggs to fledgings.

Activities

A variety of activities take place, including walks, birdwatching, fishing – both coarse and fly (permits only) – mountain biking and even parascending from the hills at the back of the centre. Contact the Clyde Muirshiel Regional Park Ranger Service (tel. 01505 614 791) or look on www.clydemuirshiel.co.uk.

Opening hours and facilities

The visitor centre is open April–Oct daily 11am–4pm and Nov–March Sat–Sun 11am–3pm. It provides maps and information, refreshments and a gift shop. The toilets, with baby changing facilities, are open daily 10am–7.45pm in summer and 10am–3.45pm in winter. Free parking and picnic areas are provided. A short 500m 'mini trail' and the first section of the Greenock Cut towpath are suitable for wheelchairs.

How to get there

By train: Glasgow Central to Inverkip or Drumfrochar (Wemyss Bay line). Inverkip is 5km from the site, so taking a bicycle might make this journey easier. Alternatively, from Drumfrochar Station, turn left and follow the road uphill past Overton Primary School. Take the second turning on your left, which leads to a small car park. From there go to the white Waterman's Cottage, through the gate and 4km along the Overton track, which leads to the visitor centre, car park and toilets. A more scenic route to the visitor centre is along the Greenock Cut (6.5km), turning right along the cut towpath instead of through the gate at the cottage. This gives great views of Greenock, the Clyde Estuary and as far as the island of Ailsa Craig.

By bus: McGill's 901 runs along the A78, from where it is a 4.5km walk uphill on a single-track road to the visitor centre.

By car: From Glasgow, take the M8/A78 through Greenock towards Inverkip and follow brown signs for the Greenock Cut Visitor Centre.

Maps: OS Landranger 63, Explorer 341.

Muirshiel Country Park

Hen harrier country with great walks and views

Grid ref: Visitor centre NS 311 631

Muirshiel Country Park covers an area of roughly 30 hectares in the West Renfrewshire Heights. The visitor centre, at the edge of heather moorland, was once the site of a Victorian shooting lodge. There are trails in mixed woodland and tracks leading out on to the moor, where you can see the remains of the 1920s' grouse railway (NS 303 674), built to transport shooting parties on to the moor, and an old barytes mine (NS 292 648). The country park, part of Clyde Muirshiel Regional Park, is surrounded by a Special Protection Area of international importance for its breeding population of hen harriers.

Within a short distance of the visitor centre you can be in heather moorland

Cuckoo.

that includes juniper. Heath spotted-orchid and bog asphodel occur in areas of boggy ground, which also has occasional carnivorous plants such as common butterwort and round-leaved sundew. Red grouse may be heard or seen from the moorland tracks, and kestrel and buzzard spotted. The headwaters of the Calder Water and other burns have dipper, grey wagtail and common sandpiper. In spring cuckoos can be heard from the visitor centre and are quite easy to spot nearby. Throughout the year, look for resident species such as raven, and visiting flocks of crossbill which may stay for a few weeks. Jays turn up occasionally as visitors, usually in autumn. More rarely, golden eagles have been seen in the area.

In May green hairstreak butterflies fly near the woodland edge among the bilberry. Several ponds provide homes for dragonflies such as the common hawker and black darter. There are very occasional sightings of common lizard scuttling along near the trails or basking on the wooden path edges.

Looking west across the moors.

© Bob Lambie

Female hen harrier and young.

Highlights

The hills surrounding the country park are home to one of the UK's rarer breeding birds, the hen harrier. The moorland offers nest sites and habitats for the animals the hen harrier eats: field voles and small birds such as meadow pipits. In April and May watch for the grey-coloured males performing their aerial display, known as 'skydancing'. Live nest camera coverage of the hen harriers can usually be seen in the visitor centre during the breeding season (May to August). You may also be lucky enough to see peregrine, short-eared owl or even merlin.

Activities

A range of activities take place, including walks, birdwatching, fly fishing (members only), mountain biking, photography and archery. For details contact the Clyde Muirshiel Regional Park Ranger Service (tel. 01505 842 803) or look on www.clydemuirshiel.co.uk.

Opening hours and facilities

The visitor centre is open April–Oct daily 11am–4pm and Nov–March Sat–Sun 11am–3pm. It provides maps and information, refreshments and a gift shop. The toilets, with baby changing facilities, are open April–Aug daily 9.30am–7.30pm, Sept–March daily 9.30am–4pm. The site has free parking and picnic areas. The area near the visitor centre, which has good views, is suitable for wheelchairs. Most trails are usable with larger-wheeled buggies.

How to get there

By train: Glasgow Central to Lochwinnoch (Ardrossan line plus a few of the trains to Ayr and Largs). The station is more than 6km away from the site, so a bicycle might ease the journey. On exiting the station, cross the A760 Largs road near the RSPB reserve, follow the off-road path for 1.5km to the Castle Semple Centre and go under the bridge and along St Winnoc Rd. Turn right on to High Street and go up the Johnshill for about 1km. Turn left on to a road signposted Muirshiel and continue for nearly 4km along the metalled road.

By bus: Take Citylink X34/X36 and get off at the Roadhead roundabout on the A737. Follow the A760 Largs road downhill to the RSPB reserve, then follow directions as given in the 'By train' section.

By car: Take the M8 past Glasgow Airport and go on to the A737, signposted Irvine. Turn on to the A760 and then the B786 through Lochwinnoch, going up the Johnshill following the brown signs for Muirshiel. The last 4km are on a single-track metalled public road.

Maps: OS Landranger 64, Explorer 341.

Castle Semple Country Park

Lochside wildlife watching and woodland walks

Grid ref: Visitor centre NS 358 591

Castle Semple Country Park, part of Clyde Muirshiel Regional Park, provides easy access to lochside strolls, views of wildlife and a wide range of outdoor activities. It is well suited to family visits. Castle Semple Loch, together with the adjacent Barr Loch, is designated a Site of Special Scientific Interest for its variety of breeding birds and rich aquatic flora.

Juvenile and adult spotted flycatchers.

Within the park, Castle Semple Loch and nearby Parkhill Wood are the remains of the Semple Estate. The Semples and succeeding landowners, MacDowalls and Harveys, left their mark on the landscape through tree planting, drainage schemes and historic built features which include the Peel Tower, Collegiate Church, a folly and fishponds.

At the loch, mute swans, mallard ducks and black-headed gulls can be seen throughout the year. Overwintering species include tufted duck and goldeneye.

By the lochside in late spring you can hear the sedge warbler, with its exotic song filled with trills and cascades interspersed with harsh chattering and mimicry, which

Castle Semple and Barr Lochs from Parkhill Wood.

is completely different to the descending sad song of the willow warbler. Blackcaps also frequent the area although they can be hard to spot in the vegetation, but their rich fluty song from the woodland understorey can help you locate their position. It is also possible to see or hear whitethroats, with their fast throaty and scratchy song, often uttered during a fluttering display flight.

The lochshore is a magnet for insect species with bumblebees and butterflies frequently seen. Orange-tips and green-veined whites are common. In summer, large numbers of swifts are sometimes seen catching insects over the water. At night pipistrelle and Daubenton's bats can be spotted feeding there. Pike and eel live in the loch, and if you are lucky you may catch sight of an otter.

At the loch edges rare plants including tufted loosestrife, creeping yellow-cress, water sedge and the scarce eight-stamened waterwort can be found, as well as commoner ones such as meadowsweet, marsh-marigolds, germander speedwell, bugle and ragged-robin. At Blackditch Bay flowering yellow water-lilies add a splash of colour.

© T Norman Tait

© Clyde Muirshiel Regional Park

© Clyde Muirshiel Regional Park

Mute swans and the visitor centre.

Parkhill Wood is a mixture of mainly native species with areas of wetter woodland where willow and birch grow. It also has a few ornamental trees, such as balsam-poplar, Turkey oak and bitternut hickory. In spring the wood is carpeted with bluebells and wood sorrel. Species indicative of ancient woodlands such as dog's mercury and wood anemone are also present. Ringlets and meadow brown butterflies can be observed over open grassy areas in midsummer.

Roe deer, brown hare, badgers and red foxes can be found in and around the woods. Birdlife includes buzzards, great spotted woodpeckers and spotted flycatchers. On summer evenings there is also a chance to see and hear male woodcock roding – engaged in special display flights to attract females.

Highlights
Castle Semple Loch has attracted many unusual birds, including red-necked phalarope, white-winged black tern, smew and more recently osprey, which are occasionally seen flying over the loch and even fishing in the summer months.

Activities
There is a maze in Parkhill Wood, fashioned from an area of dense rhododendron. Other activities include walking, cycling (National Cycle Route 7), birdwatching, fishing (by permit), kayaking, canoeing, sailing, outdoor activity courses and taster sessions, which must be booked in advance, and boat and bike hire (charges apply). For more details contact the Clyde Muirshiel Regional Park Ranger Service or the Outdoor Instructors (tel. 01505 842 882) or look on www. clydemuirshiel.co.uk.

Opening hours and facilities
Castle Semple Visitor Centre is open April–Oct daily 10am–5pm, Nov–March daily 10am–4pm. It provides maps and information, refreshments, a gift shop, showers and changing rooms, including ones with wheelchair access and babychanging facilities. The toilets are open April–Oct daily 9am–8pm, Nov–March daily 9am–4pm. There is free parking and picnic areas are provided. The visitor centre and lochside trails, which are on level tarmacked surfaces, are wheelchair accessible.

How to get there
By bicycle: Sustrans National Cycle Route 7 passes the visitor centre, Parkhill Wood and the Collegiate Church.

By train: Glasgow Central to Lochwinnoch (Ardrossan line, plus a few of the trains to Ayr and Largs). Exit the station and cross the A760 Largs road near the RSPB reserve. Follow the off-road path around the loch for about 1.5km. The path is level and tarmacked.

By bus: Take Citylink X34/X36, and get off at the Roadhead roundabout on the A737. Follow the A760 Largs road downhill to the RSPB reserve, and then follow the off-road path around the loch for about 1.5km.

By car: Take the M8 past Glasgow Airport on to the A737, signposted Irvine. Follow the brown signs for Castle Semple.

Maps: OS Landranger 63, Explorer 341.

Lochwinnoch RSPB Reserve

Otters, nearly 200 species of birds and family-friendly nature trails

Grid ref: Car park NS 358 580

Lochwinnoch RSPB Reserve was established in 1973 and comprises 159 hectares of wetland, wet grassland and woodland. It is within Clyde Muirshiel Regional Park, and part of the Castle Semple and Barr lochs Site of Special Scientific Interest.

There are recorded sightings of 195 species of birds, more than 20 species of mammals, five species of dragonflies, 15 species of butterflies and over 110 species of moths, including some local rarities such as Haworth's minor and small square-spot moths.

In the spring and summer a wide range of wetland and woodland birds can be observed, including many summer migrants. A cacophony of birdsong in the woodland will greet you, as a mixture of resident and migrant species attempt to 'out sing' each other. In the summer the reeling and screeching from sedge and grasshopper warblers is also well worth a listen. Other migrant species include blackcap, whitethroat, spotted flycatcher and chiffchaff.

At the end of autumn the reserve changes, and overwintering wildfowl start to arrive: during the winter months large numbers are present on one or more of the bodies of water in the area – in some years, very large numbers, particularly when there is an abundance of pondweed, which the birds eat. One recent winter more than 550 wigeon, 400 coot, 400 tufted ducks and over 100 goldeneye were recorded.

The reserve feeding stations are very popular – both with birds and birdwatchers. Visiting birds range from commonly seen species such as robins, blue tits, starlings and chaffinches, to less common species such as great spotted woodpecker, lesser redpoll and even occasional water rail, brambling and fieldfare. Keep your eyes peeled for bank voles attracted by the food – and weasels, attracted by the voles. Roe deer are quite common on the reserve and red foxes are occasionally seen.

Aird Meadow Loch, Lochwinnoch RSPB Reserve.

© Andy Hay (rspb-images.com)

© Chris Everett

© Tom Marshall (rspb-images.com)

Above: Great spotted woodpecker.

Above right: Otter.

Highlights

The reserve is one of the best places for otters in the greater Clyde area, with regular sightings. Bird highlights can include whooper swans, the elusive smew, and hen harriers hunting over the Aird Meadow.

Activities

There is an extensive programme throughout the year. Typical activities include bat and moth walks, the school holiday club, nest-box building, guided walks and seasonal events such as Fright Night, Festive Fun and Easter Eggstravaganza. The reserve runs activities for children and families daily, including the monthly wildlife challenge and bird bingo (all year), plus pond dipping and bug hunting (April–October). Indoor events are run when the weather is poor. For more details phone 01505 842 663 or see www. rspb.org.uk/lochwinnoch.

Facilities

The reserve visitor centre, with shop, is open daily from 10am–5pm. It is wheelchair accessible, and an accessible toilet is located next to the visitor centre. The reserve has two wheelchair-friendly visitor trails: one runs through marshland and alongside the Dubbs Water, and the other has two accessible birdwatching hides, which give excellent views of the Aird Meadow Loch, and runs thorough some beautiful mixed deciduous woodland before finally reaching a viewpoint overlooking Castle Semple Loch. There is a small charge to go round the trails and hides, but this is waived if you have come to the reserve on foot, by bicycle or by public transport, or are a member of the RSPB or Wildlife Explorers. The reserve also has a popular small hide for photographing garden birds. It can get very busy, so it is best to check ahead – to do so or for more information phone the reserve on 01505 842 663.

How to get there

By bicycle: Sustrans National Cycle Route 7 runs through the reserve, adjacent to the A737.

By train: Glasgow Central to Lochwinnoch (Ardrossan line, plus a few of the trains to Ayr and Largs). The reserve is 300m north-west of the station.

By bus: Take Citylink X34/X36 and get off at the Roadhead roundabout on the A737 (NS 350 586), 750m south-east of the reserve entrance.

By car: Take the M8 past Glasgow Airport and continue on to the A737, signposted Irvine. Turn right at the A760, and follow brown signs for RSPB Nature Centre. Car parking facilities are available.

Maps: OS Landranger 63, Explorer 341.

Clyde Estuary

An area of international importance for birds

Grid refs: Park Quay for Newshot Island NS 474 707; West Ferry NS 404 730; Parklea NS 352 740

As the River Clyde nears the open sea, it widens into an estuary with a variety of habitats – extensive intertidal mudflats fringed by stretches of reedbed, saltmarsh and rocky shore. This is an important area for wildlife, and the invertebrates and fish produced by this fertile ecosystem provide food for large numbers of shorebirds and waterbirds. For this reason, most of the Clyde Estuary is classified as a Site of Special Scientific Interest and as a Special Protection Area because of its important population of redshank.

The intertidal mudflats often support extensive patches of dwarf eel grass and sea lettuce, both important food plants for a number of wildfowl species. Various other intertidal plants occur throughout the estuary, including serrated wrack, which is abundant on stony mudflats and on extensive mussel beds such as at Pillar Bank off Cardross.

Invertebrates on and within the mudflats support not only the birds for which the Clyde Estuary is renowned, but

Greenshank.

© David Palmar (www.photoscot.co.uk)

also fish, including flounder, thick-lipped grey mullet and sprat. Runs of sea trout and Atlantic salmon occur at various times of the year. In the lower reaches of the estuary, as it approaches the Firth of Clyde, Atlantic herring and mackerel are seasonally abundant, and butterfish tend to inhabit kelp beds. In recent years fish have become more plentiful as oxygen levels in the estuary have improved.

The increase in fish has led to a rise in the number of fish-eating birds, especially red-throated diver, cormorant, shag and guillemot. Even flocks of the usually oceanic Manx shearwater have been seen feeding off Greenock in recent years, mainly during July and August.

The populations of red-throated diver and cormorant, and also of eider, goldeneye, red-breasted merganser, great crested grebe, oystercatcher, curlew and black-headed gull are of national importance. The estuary supports an internationally important winter population of redshank. Wintering Slavonian grebes – mainly off Ardmore Point (p. **84**) on the north side of the estuary – are sometimes present in internationally significant numbers.

Saltmarshes, which mostly occur at the upper reaches of the river, are often dominated by red fescue and other salt-tolerant grasses, and flowering plants including sea club-rush, saltmarsh rush, sea aster, common scurvy grass and spear-leaved orache. There are extensive reedbeds of common reed at Newshot Island and to the east of Longhaugh Point (NS 430 730).

Waders gather to roost communally at high tide, and the best time for watching them is as they disperse to feeding areas as the tide drops (two–three hours after

© Iain P Gibson

The Clyde Estuary from the Erskine Bridge.

actual high tide). The following sites on the southern shore of the Clyde are fairly easy to access.

Newshot Island Local Nature Reserve, near Erskine, is a good place to see redshank from autumn to spring, common sandpiper in spring and summer, and the rarer greenshank in autumn to winter. Less common migrant species, such as ruff or black-tailed godwit, pass through in autumn. There is a viewing point with a screened platform at Park Quay. It looks out over the mouth of the saltmarsh creek. Further up this creek is a lagoon with surrounding reedbeds. Although access is difficult, water rails with young can be seen in late summer, and up to 10,000 swallows gather to roost at dusk (best in August/early September).

West Ferry, near Langbank, is a good place from which to view extensive mudflats – ideally with binoculars or a telescope. During winter large flocks of common waders – oystercatcher, lapwing, curlew and redshank – can be observed. Wildfowl include teal, wigeon and shelduck. During the second half of April, around 50 black-tailed godwit may be seen between West Ferry and Longhaugh Point to the east, and over 300 have been recorded. The mudflats

here constitute an important nursery and feeding area for shelduck in summer. In late April and early May, whimbrel, a smaller relative of the curlew, come to the shore east of the car park. Most years hundreds of goldeneye, and up to 70 scaup, congregate to feed offshore during April and early May.

Parklea, to the east of Port Glasgow, is worth visiting during autumn and winter. Walk east along the shore from the car park by the playing fields to see up to ten or more greenshank, large flocks of redshank and a

Redshank.

© David Palmar (www.photoscot.co.uk)

137

Lugworm casts in the mudflats at South Bay, Ardmore Point.

variety of wildfowl including red-breasted merganser and wigeon in the Finlaystone Point area (NS 353 741).

Highlights

The Clyde is a regular wintering site for greenshank, which are quite rare in Scotland in winter, with up to 12 birds between Parklea and Finlaystone Point, and several singles elsewhere including Newshot Island. They feed on various invertebrates such as young shore crabs, which they catch in small pools on the mudflats.

Black-tailed godwit and whimbrel, stopping off on their journey north to Iceland, occur on passage in late April/early May and again in August/September. In spring the godwits are usually in superb breeding plumage, with rich orange-red chests, whereas autumn migrants tend to be juvenile birds with warm buff tones in their plumage. Feeding strategies differ between species: black-tailed godwits probe the mud deeply with their long, straight bills and feed mainly on ragworms, whereas whimbrels, despite having long curved bills, delicately pick small snails and crustaceans, including young shore crabs, from the surface of the mud or rocks.

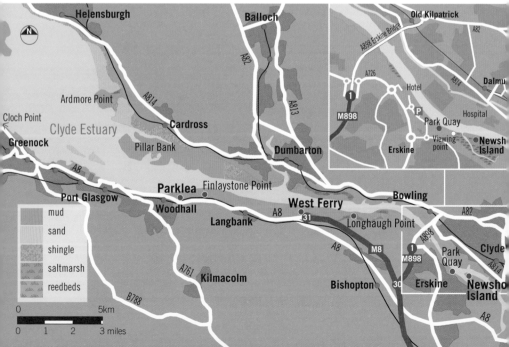

Also nearby
Cloch Point (NS 204 760), near Gourock, is a good place to watch offshore seabirds, especially from July to September. Manx shearwaters may be seen in flocks of hundreds, and look out for gannets, black guillemots, sandwich terns, and scarcer passage seabirds such as arctic skua and great skua.

Note: The shoreline varies in how suitable it is for walking along, and it is important when planning a walk to know the time of high tide. (See www.bbc.co.uk/weather/coast and select Tide tables, then Scotland, then Greenock, Port Glasgow or Bowling.)

Newshot Island: Extreme care is needed when accessing the saltmarsh, due to the rough and marshy nature of the ground, and access should *not* be attempted three hours either side of high tide.

Longhaugh Point–West Ferry: It is possible to walk along this part of the shore *except* during one-and-a-half hours either side of high tide.

West Ferry–Parklea: This stretch is another potential walk, though sections between West Ferry and Langbank and Langbank and Finlaystone Point are only accessible at low or on a falling tide. Do *not* attempt during three hours either side of high tide.

How to get there

On foot:
Park Quay for Newshot Island can be reached along the riverside footpath from Erskine town centre.

By train:
West Ferry: Glasgow Central to Langbank (Gourock line), then follow the pavement east along Main Rd for 2km to Junction 31 of the M8, where you can cross under the M8 flyover. Alternatively, though it involves a much longer walk, Glasgow Central to Bishopton (Gourock line), from where you can follow the A8, B815 and walk past Erskine Golf Course to Longhaugh Point, and then along the shore to West Ferry.

Parklea: Glasgow Central to Woodhall (Gourock line). Exit the station on the north side of the line, turn right and walk along Kelburn Terrace to the A8 underpass just before the roundabout which takes you down to Parklea. Or, Glasgow Central to Langbank, from where, at low or falling tide, you can walk to Parklea.

By bus:
Newshot Island: Arriva bus X23 to the Bridgewater Shopping Centre, Erskine. From here cross the zebra crossing and follow the path parallel to Newshot Drive for about 300m to the LNR entrance. The viewing point is another 200m from the entrance.

West Ferry and *Parklea:* McGill's 901, 906 and 907 buses pass nearby, close to the stations Langbank and Woodhall. For West Ferry, follow the directions given in 'By train'. For Parklea get off at the first stop after the roundabout where the bus leaves the A8. Then follow the railway/A8 underpass near the roundabout which takes you to Parklea.

By car:
Newshot Island: Follow the M8 west to Junction 30, take the M898 (Erskine Bridge road) and take the first exit. At the roundabout turn right and follow the A726. Turn left at the second main roundabout (signposted Erskine Swimming Pool). Turn left at the next roundabout and after about 300m there is parking on the right. Walk east along the Clyde walkway for about 600m to get to the viewing point. Alternately, park at the Bridgewater shopping centre and walk east along the pavement for 300m to the Newshot Drive entrance to the LNR.

West Ferry: Follow the M8 west to Junction 31 for Bishopton, and at the roundabout turn right (signposted West Ferry). There is a car park immediately to the right.

Parklea: Take the M8 west from Glasgow and continue along the A8 past Langbank and Finlaystone. At the next roundabout turn right (signposted Kelburn Park and Parklea), and then right again. Drive along the minor road until you arrive at the car park by the playing fields.

Maps: Glasgow street map (partial coverage); OS Landranger 63 and 64, Explorer 342 and 347.

Glen Moss

Undisturbed wetland habitat with dragonflies and damselflies

Grid ref: Entrance NS 363 697

Glen Moss is a wetland site of roughly 20 hectares, which lies in a natural hollow in the Renfrewshire hills, 150 metres above sea level and about 500m east of Kilmacolm. The site was marked as 'bog' on a map of 1796; today it is best described as a mixed basin and valley mire with an area of shallow open water surrounded by sedge-dominated plant communities. Such a naturally occurring and undisturbed wetland habitat is uncommon, and in 1973 Glen Moss was designated as a Site of Special Scientific Interest. In 1991 the Scottish Wildlife Trust negotiated with local landowners the right to treat the southern area of Glen Moss as a Nature Reserve.

During the Ice Age, glaciers moved east-south-east across the area and gouged out the softer rocks to form a shallow glacial lake. The site's underlying basalt rocks are impermeable and this has resulted in Glen Moss being a marshy wetland for many centuries. Springs in the north and east flow into the area, providing a throughput of fresh water.

The wide range of habitats found throughout the SSSI support diverse plant life, and more than 200 species have been recorded, a number of which are locally rare. Examples include tufted loosetrife and bog sedge, which grow throughout the marshy parts of the site. The inconspicuous coralroot orchid may be found growing through carpets of moss under willow scrub, which surrounds the reserve. In springtime flowering broom and gorse add splashes of vibrant yellow, and rafts of pink-flowering bogbean brighten the open water. In summer the white tufts of bog-cotton seed heads waft in the breeze, and in autumn the dying flowers of bog asphodel give a brilliant reddish colour to the marshy margins around the open water.

Four types of dragonfly and five types of damselfly breed at the reserve, making Glen Moss a very important site for these insects. The first to come into view, around late April, is the large red damselfly, followed in May by the four-spotted chaser dragonfly and the common blue damselfly. During July, common and black darter dragonflies make an appearance and emerald and blue-tailed damselflies emerge from the boggy pools. The most spectacular dragonfly to look out for is the common hawker, which is about 10cm from wing tip to

Open water at Glen Moss.

© T Norman Tait

wing tip. Despite its large size, this insect is completely harmless to humans and cannot sting or bite. All of these insects catch and eat smaller insects.

In summer butterflies abound at marshy edges of the water, and there are at least eight breeding species here. The first to appear, in early May, is the easily overlooked green hairstreak. In June and July the beautiful small pearl-bordered fritillary may be seen feeding on the opening flowers of marsh thistles. Ringlets, recent arrivals at Glen Moss, and meadow browns flit through the grassy areas and willow warblers and reed buntings sing throughout the site.

In winter the reserve is silent except for the tinkling call of teal duck as they fly. Tufted duck, wigeon and goosander are often seen resting and feeding at the edge of the open water.

© T Norman Tait

Female common hawker dragonfly.

Highlights

For the botanist there are many uncommon wetland plants. The insect lover can look out for dragonflies, damselflies, butterflies, hoverflies and bumblebees. In addition, there are panoramic views and a tranquil environment to enjoy.

Coralroot orchid.

© T Norman Tait

Activities

Occasional outings during the summer months are led by the Scottish Wildlife Trust – for details see www.clydeswt.org.

Facilities

To assist access to the site by the public, the SWT has put in place a series of paths and boardwalks, though slopes and steps make these unsuitable for wheelchairs.

How to get there

By train: Glasgow Central to Johnstone (Ardrossan line): the station is about 10km away from the site.

By bus: McGill's City Connect X7 and Slaemuir Coaches X7 both run via Kilmacolm Cross: alight here and walk across Bridge of Weir Rd into Moss Rd and then right into Gillburn Rd, right into Gowkhouse Rd and proceed uphill on the unsurfaced Gowkhouse Lane. Follow the lane up to Glenmosston Rd and enter the reserve along the signposted right-of-way.

By car: Take the A761 from Paisley to Kilmacolm. On entering Kilmacolm take the second right into Porterfield Rd (follow the signs for the golf course) and second left into Rowantreehill Rd. Glenmosston Rd is first on the right. Restricted parking space is available on the right-hand side at the reserve entrance near the end of Glenmosston Rd.

Maps: OS Landranger 63, Explorer 341.

Paisley Moss

A wetland nature reserve next to Glasgow Airport

Grid refs: St Andrew's Drive entrance NS 473 657; centre of site NS 469 656

Paisley Moss lies between Junction 28 of the M8 motorway and Glasgow Airport. It gets its name from 'the Great Moss' which once extended over the floodplains of the Black Cart Water and River Gryfe, between Paisley and Houston; the existing site is a tiny remnant covering four hectares. Although strictly it is no longer a moss, as most of the surface peatland has been lost, the small wetland reserve has a remarkable diversity of habitats. The site is owned by BAA, and managed by a partnership between BAA, Renfrewshire Council, Scottish Natural Heritage and the Scottish Ornithologists' Club. It is a Local Nature Reserve and a Site of Importance for Nature Conservation.

The main wetland area is dominated by sedges: 11 species have been recorded, including bottle sedge, water sedge and slender tufted-sedge. There is also a good diversity of other aquatic plant species, such as marsh cinquefoil, mare's-tail, water horsetail and water plantain. Around the sedge swamp are patches of mire vegetation with some bog mosses, including a small

area with round-leaved sundew. Some tall herbs and aquatic plants are encroaching on the mire, most notably bulrush – a relatively recent arrival that has become dominant over a large area. The locally uncommon adder's-tongue fern is found in grassland in the south-east corner. Scrub woodland at the site is an important element of biodiversity, with older willows supporting an interesting community of lichens.

There is a wealth of invertebrate life at the site. 'Pond dipping' at the small areas of open water produces many aquatic invertebrates, including both the larvae and adults of the spectacular great diving beetle, and damselfly larvae, the adults of which fly around the reserve in summer. Several species of butterfly occur, including orange-tips in May, and impressive elephant hawkmoth caterpillars can occasionally be found on rosebay willowherb.

Over 80 species of birds have been recorded at the site. Common snipe are plentiful on autumn migration, especially

Paisley Moss, just south of Glasgow Airport's runway.

Jack snipe.

Common snipe.

in October – sometimes 30 or more are present. Reed bunting and sedge warbler breed here in summer, and occasionally a male grasshopper warbler can be detected by its prolonged trilling song. Water rails are present in winter, and it is thought there may be a breeding pair.

Visitors may also see common frog and palmate newt, several small mammal species, red foxes and roe deer.

Highlights

Paisley Moss is one of the best places in Scotland for finding the elusive jack snipe, a passage migrant and winter visitor from northern Europe. It is cryptically plumaged, which helps it stay camouflaged, and it will crouch in marshland vegetation until almost stood upon before rising – which it does with very little sound, usually landing again not far away. The larger common snipe is more easily disturbed, repeatedly utters a harsh '*schep*' call, and flies off into the distance with a very rapid and often zigzag flight. Jack snipe frequent the marshiest parts of the site, so if trying to locate them wellingtons are essential.

Also nearby

The Black Cart Water SPA at Inchinnan (NS 476 679) is significant for its internationally important flock of Icelandic whooper swans, which come to the area between October and April, with peak numbers usually present in late November or early December.

Facilities

A circular path runs right around the reserve, including a wheelchair-friendly boardwalk with viewing platforms round the southern and western sides. A leaflet about the reserve is available: phone 0141 842 5811/5822 or email pt@renfrewshire.gov.uk.

How to get there

On foot or by bicycle: The Glasgow Airport to Inchinnan cycle route and path passes through the site.

By train: Glasgow Central to Paisley Gilmour Street. Then take Arriva bus 66, which runs to the airport every 10 minutes.

By bus: Arriva bus 500 to Glasgow Airport Terminal Building. Paisley Moss is a 10-minute walk away. Follow directions on the blue signposts for the Inchinnan cycle route and Paisley Moss Nature Reserve.

By car: From Glasgow take the M8 to Glasgow Airport (Junction 28). Go under the M8, turn left at the roundabout, then left again into the small business estate (signposted authorized buses and taxis only). At the next T-junction, turn left following the small sign to Paisley Moss Nature Reserve. Continue to the end of St Andrew's Drive, where there is space for a couple of cars to park beyond the double yellow lines. From here a short path leads into the reserve.

Maps: Glasgow Street map; OS Landranger 64, Explorer 342.

Gleniffer Braes Country Park

An upland country park with a rare breeding bird

Grid refs: Robertson car park NS 455 606; Brownside Farm car park NS 488 606

Gleniffer Braes Country Park lies to the south of Paisley on the Gleniffer and Brownside braes. It covers an area of about 480 hectares, 4.5km wide by 1.5km. This upland country park mainly consists of moorland but it also has forested parts and hill farming areas. There are very impressive views north across the Clyde Valley towards the Kilpatrick Hills, and on a clear day as far as Ben Lomond.

The country park is located on the edge of the lavas of the Clyde Plateau Volcanic Formation (see p. 17). One of its most interesting parts is the Gleniffer Gorge (NS 463 605), on the Tannahill Way. This reaches about 15m deep in places, and is eroded by the Gleniffer Burn, which runs along a fault and cuts through the lavas. Another attraction is the outstanding waterfall in Glen Park, where long icicles can be seen hanging in winter.

The entire length of the braes slope is an important landscape feature and includes much habitat of nature conservation interest. The country park is a mixture of very diverse habitats, including unimproved grasslands, from strongly acidic to neutral, and heath, wetlands, burns, open water, mire, scrub and woodlands. Such a wide variety of habitats produces a complex area of high diversity.

Many of the botanical highlights are found in the fields grazed by Highland cattle and are dependent on this land management for their survival. Mountain pansy can be found in summer and rare colourful waxcap fungi are best looked for in late summer and early autumn. The moonwort fern is a locally very rare species which has been seen at a couple of spots on the braes. Greater butterfly orchids are one of the most strikingly beautiful floral contributions. They can be seen in significant numbers during June in the Brownside Braes area (NS 483 606).

The country park in general hosts typical woodland fauna such as blue tit, goldcrest and chaffinch, roe deer and red fox. Up in the moorland, skylark and

Opposite: Waterfall, Glen Park.

Below: Highland cattle on the braes – their grazing helps maintain the habitat.

© Patricia Brown

Lesser whitethroat.

© Tom Byars

meadow pipit can be seen, and kestrels hunting for voles and shrews are not uncommon.

Highlights

This is one of the country's most northern breeding sites for the lesser whitethroat – a small warbler which spends the winter in the Nile Valley and Ethiopian highlands before heading to the UK in the spring. If you are very lucky you may catch a glimpse of this bird in the early spring, but you are more likely to hear the male singing around his

territory in the hope of attracting a mate. As the bird requires very dense hawthorn scrub with thick brambles underneath to breed successfully, there is a scrub creation and management project within the Brownside Braes area.

Activities

Renfrewshire Council's Land Services

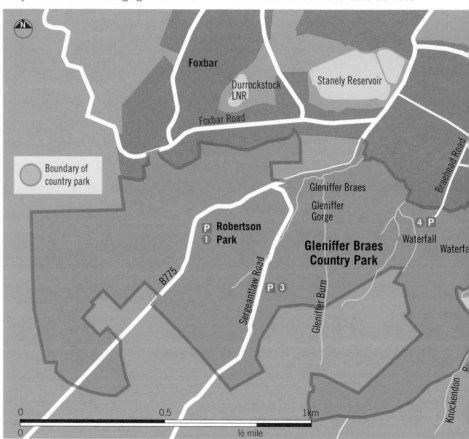

Officers run guided walks and activities – for more information, phone them at Glen Lodge on 0141 884 3794 or see www.renfrewshire. gov.uk.

Also nearby

Durrockstock LNR (NS 456 615) lies just to the north in Foxbar. At the eastern and southern ends of the reserve there is woodland and dense wet scrub and a small reed bed. The wildlife interest is largely birdlife, including tufted duck and grey heron. Pike and common toad are also present.

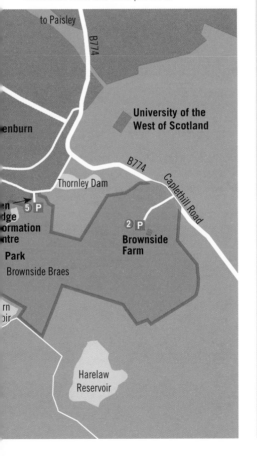

Facilities

There is an information centre at Glen Lodge, with toilets, though these are only accessible when the Land Services Officers are at the lodge. Seats and picnic tables are available at Robertson Park car park. A very limited area is suitable for wheelchairs – the 800m mixed pedestrian and cycle path from the entrance track of Brownside Braes to Glenfield Rd.

How to get there

By train: Glasgow Central to Paisley Gilmour Street, about 3–5km away from the country park with the option taking a bus (see 'By bus' below), or Glasgow Central to Barrhead (Barrhead and Kilmarnock lines), about a 3km walk from the Brownside Braes area. From Barrhead Station, walk up Graham St, then turn right on to Hillside Rd – at the end this becomes a track, and the park is signposted. Follow the track north-west towards Harelaw Dam, from where there are tracks heading north-east up through the golf course and on to Brownside Braes. This route covers fairly steep terrain on informal paths, so walking boots or wellingtons are recommended.

By bus: From Paisley, Arriva 1 from Gauze St or McGill's 54 from Brick Lane. In both cases, alight at the Caplethill Rd stop opposite Glenfield Rd. Go down Glenfield Rd and the entrance to the site is the third on the left, about 400m away.

By car: From Paisley, head south on the B774. Turn right on to the B775 (signposted Lugton and Irvine), and follow this road, which is fairly steep in places, until it goes up the braes. Robertson car park (1) is the second turning on the left. Alternatively, from Paisley stay on the B774 to Brownside Farm (2), about 400m after the University of the West of Scotland campus, where there is a small car park down the track on the right. Parking is also available at Sergeantlaw Rd (3), Braehead Rd (4) and Glen Park (5).

Maps: Glasgow street map (partial coverage); OS Landranger 64, Explorer 342.

Loch Libo

A loch with rare aquatic plants and water voles

Grid ref: Entrance and parking NS 437 558

Loch Libo Reserve, established in 1973 by the Scottish Wildlife Trust, is in the valley of the Lugton Water next to the East Renfrewshire town of Uplawmoor. The 18-hectare site comprises a long, shallow freshwater loch and a hillside cloaked in mature deciduous woodland. The reserve is the best nutrient-rich loch in East Renfrewshire and is a Site of Special Scientific Interest.

There is a path that can be followed to the woodland to walk in the shade of tall sycamore, beech and ash trees. Young trees and a carpet of ferns and mosses give the place a lush and leafy feel. There are no paths to the loch shore but it is worth cutting down through the woodland to stand beside the water and scan it for wildlife. You will, however, need your wellies to do so as the many springs keep the ground water-logged throughout the year.

Rare aquatic plants are found in the loch's perimeter sedge swamps and reedbeds (it is these that give the reserve

Bogbean.

© T Norman Tait

its SSSI status). Huge pedestals of greater tussock sedge are visible beneath the aspen trees at the end of the loch near the entrance. Four other unusual sedges are present, along with other challenges for the specialist botanist, and there are also more distinctive plants for recreational flower spotters to enjoy. For example, the ferny leaves and large white flower heads of cowbane – nationally scarce, and deadly poisonous – lurk among the reeds and sedges in several places around the loch shore. Although it has not been seen for many years, the rare crested buckler fern used to be found at Loch Libo – there is no other known Scottish location for this species.

Winter visits to the loch can be rewarded by sightings of good numbers of waterfowl, such as wigeon, goldeneye, teal, tufted duck and, if you are lucky, whooper swan. In the spring the mature woodland overlooking the loch is alive with common songbirds, thanks

Loch Libo.

© Jody Warner

to the abundance of nest sites and insects. Fungi are everywhere in autumn, both on the woodland floor and on the many fallen trees deliberately left for them to grow on. Signs of otters are regularly found around the loch – they scent-mark their territory and make tracks as they enter the reserve to catch fish in the loch. Carp, roach, tench, perch and pike are all present.

The geology of the general area around Loch Libo is formed by Carboniferous lavas of the Clyde Plateau Volcanic Formation (See p. 17). However, the valley in which the loch lies has been eroded along two faults, between which there is a wedge of Carboniferous sedimentary rocks. These are mainly sandstone with some coal seams, which were mined near the loch in the late eighteenth century. At the waterfall of the west burn (NS 432 557) the sandstone is exposed lying vertically against the basalt lava.

© T Norman Tait

Water vole.

Highlights

The presence of water voles was confirmed in 2009. The water vole is Britain's most endangered mammal. Its dramatic decline over the last 50 years is attributed mainly to predation by the American mink, although habitat fragmentation, disturbance and pollution have played their part. This makes this large, peaceful and clean loch all the more important. The presence of otters is also said to discourage mink. Water voles eat the leaves and roots of waterside plants and make burrows in the sides of watercourses.

Activities

There are occasional Scottish Wildlife Trust guided walks – see www.swt.org.uk or phone 01294 279 376. Only members of the Scottish Carp Group are permitted to fish at the loch.

Also nearby

The Irvine Greenspaces are further south along the A736 – nine more SWT Wildlife Reserves. These sites are highly accessible and offer a surprising range of habitats to explore: see www.swt.org.uk for more information.

Facilities

There is a way-marked path, though this is not surfaced and can be muddy.

How to get there

By bus: Stagecoach X44B: alight just past Uplawmoor at Caldwell Golf Course and very carefully walk back along the grass verge to the reserve entrance – or, better, ask to be dropped there.

By car: From Paisley, take the A736 through Barrhead and Neilston towards Uplawmoor. About 1km after Shillford you will see a pedestrian railway crossing on the right. Park in the lay-by 100m further on, also on the right. Take special care walking along the grass verge and crossing the railway.

Maps: OS Landranger 64, Explorer 342; a reserve map is available to download from www.swt.org.uk.

Rouken Glen Park

A formal park with lots of wild corners

Grid refs: Main entrance NS 548 586; East Lodge car park NS 551 584; south-east entrance NS 553 577

Much of Rouken Glen Park, near Thornliebank, is formally managed parkland. However, the middle section of the glen itself is a spectacular area of woodland landscape. The park is designated as a Site of Importance for Nature Conservation, and a narrow strip of land along the Auldhouse Burn, extending almost the entire length through the park, is designated as a Site of Special Scientific Interest.

The site is of national significance for geology because, when studied together with Waulkmill Glen (see p. 74), the two sites show the best examples in central Scotland of a particular sequence of sedimentary rocks. These date from the Upper Limestone Formation (uppermost

The waterfall and Giffnock Sandstone.

Lower Carboniferous age) – from about 320 million years ago, when Scotland was close to the equator, on the southern edge of a major continent. Part of the section is exposed at Rouken Glen but obscured in Waulkmill Glen. This, along with the absence of geological faults here (which indicates an unbroken and therefore uncomplicated rock sequence) makes Rouken Glen very important. Both sites show sedimentary and fossil differences and variations within these rock layers.

There is also evidence of the last Ice Age to be found in the park. The flattish rocks next to the southern edge of the boating pond were smoothed by glacial action and gouged with scratch marks, known as 'striae', when rock fragments were dragged over the rocks by glaciers.

More than 170 species of native and naturalized vascular plants have been recorded at the park, including some uncommon species such as greater butterfly-orchid, giant bellflower, large bittercress, wood horsetail, hard shield-fern and curled pondweed. The trees are a mixture of native and non-native species, with native sessile oak, pedunculate oak, ash, wych elm and silver birch growing beside the introduced Norway spruce, cypress and Corsican pine.

Wet rocky outcrops adjacent to the burn support a good variety of mosses and ferns, including hart's-tongue fern. The sides and banks of the burn have become colonized by many exotic plants, particularly rhododendron, but also berberis, snowberry and bamboo. The wooded stretches either side of the burn include remnants of ground flora from the original woodland, such as wood-sedge, sanicle, wood melick, wood sorrel, common dog violet, dog's mercury, common woodruff and wood sage.

Boating pond with mute swans and cygnets.

Hart's-tongue fern.

Over 70 species of birds have been recorded within the park, and of these 34 probably nest here, including song thrush, spotted flycatcher, starling and bullfinch. The boating pond, which has small islands with trees, attracts mallard, tufted duck, mute swan, coot and black-headed gulls. Dipper, kingfisher and grey wagtail have been recorded feeding along the Auldhouse Burn, which supports fish such as minnow, stone loach, three-spined stickleback and brown trout. Red fox and grey squirrel are common in the park, pipistrelle bats are regularly seen by evening visitors and badgers and otters have also been recorded.

Highlights

The rocks at the waterfall and the nearby 'picnic rocks', are Giffnock Sandstone, which was quarried locally and used for many buildings in Glasgow.

Activities

Occasional walks and other activities are organized by the Friends of Rouken Glen Park. For further information contact Steve Edwards: phone 0141 842 5272 or email steveedwards56@hotmail.com.

Facilities

There are toilets, including wheelchair-accessible ones, a visitor centre (open May–Sept Mon–Fri 9am–5pm, Sat–Sun 9am–4.30pm; Oct–April 9am–4pm), a café (open 8.30am–5.00pm in winter and 8.30am–7.00pm in summer), boats to hire, a garden centre, a children's play area, information boards and colour-coded routes for walkers and joggers. Phone 0141 638 7411 for more information. Most paths are suitable for wheelchairs, although there are steps beside the waterfall.

How to get there

By train: Glasgow Central to Whitecraigs (Neilston line), adjacent to the park entrance.

By bus: First bus 38A/38C passes the entrances to the park on Rouken Glen Rd.

By car: From Glasgow follow the A77 to Eastwood Toll roundabout. Turn right here on to the A726, from where you can drive to one of three places to park. For the first, turn left at the traffic lights and go down Davieland Rd for 500m – there is parking at the side of the road beside the south-east entrance. For the second, keep on the A726 and park in the East Lodge car park, on the left just after Davieland Rd. For the third, continue for another 250m to the main entrance and car park, which is on the left.

Maps: Glasgow street map; OS Landranger 64, Explorer 342; British Geological Survey S30E Glasgow and S22E Kilmarnock.

South and east

To the south and east of the city there are ancient oaks, gorge woodlands with rare beetles, breeding peregrines, uncommon butterflies, colourful fungi and spectacular waterfalls.

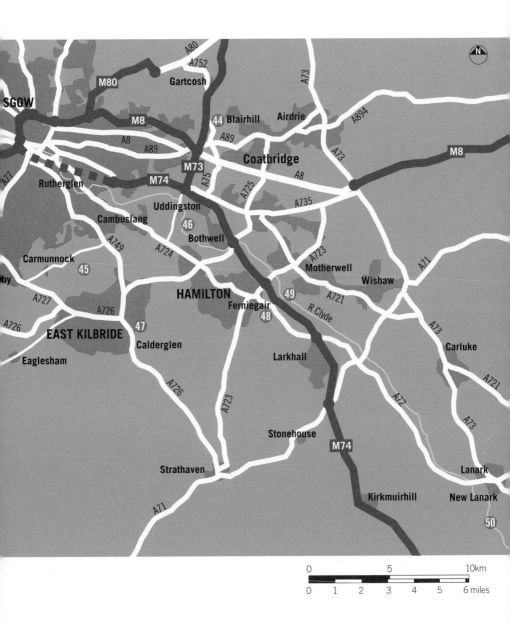

Drumpellier Country Park

Lochs, a disused canal and a good place to see butterflies

Grid ref: Visitor centre NS 704 664

Drumpellier Country Park is to the east of Glasgow and just north-west of Coatbridge. Extending over 202 hectares, the park is centred around Woodend and Lochend lochs and also contains a large section of the Monkland Canal, ponds, woodland, heathland, grassland and a raised bog. In Lochend Loch there is the remains of a crannog, a man-made island and defensive dwelling dating from around 100 BC. The land was given to be a public park by the Buchanan family in 1919. It was designated as a Country Park in 1984, and is managed by North Lanarkshire Council. Woodend Loch is designated as a Site of Special Scientific Interest.

The two lochs were formed about 11,500 years ago at the end of the last Ice Age and are believed to be kettle holes (depressions formed by retreating glaciers). They are part of a chain of lochs which also includes Hogganfield, Frankfield and Bishop lochs (see pp. 66–71).

The park from the air: Lochend Loch on the left, Woodend Loch on the right.

A wide variety of plants are found within the park. In 2008, some 59 species of mosses and liverworts were recorded within the raised bog habitat, including sphagnum mosses and the carnivorous round-leaved sundew. Orchids grow in the park, including broad-leaved helleborine and early purple orchid.

Woodend Loch has rich aquatic plant life and overwintering wildfowl. Reed buntings and sedge warblers often appear around the loch edges in warmer months. In spring, swifts, swallows and martins feed above the water in their hundreds.

The native broadleaved woodlands are a place to spot fungi in autumn, and are also popular areas for nesting jays and raptors such as buzzards and sparrowhawks. Water rail can be seen on the edges of West Pond by Lochend Loch.

The raised bog is a good place for watching dragonflies in summer, and Daubenton's bats feed above the lochs on summer evenings.

© North Lanarkshire Council

Small pearl-bordered fritillary feeding on marsh thistle.

© Richard Sutcliffe

Highlights

The park is a hot spot for butterflies – especially small pearl-bordered fritillaries, which can be seen close to the M73. The comma butterfly was first recorded at Drumpellier in 2008.

Activities

There are guided walks and activities led by North Lanarkshire Countryside Rangers throughout the year. A free 'Greenspace Diary' can be obtained from the visitor centre and at www.northlanarkshire.gov.uk. Fishing for coarse fish on the canal or rainbow trout on Lochend Loch is permitted. No fishing is allowed on Woodend Loch.

Also nearby

Gartcosh Nature Reserve (NS 705 683), 2km to the north, has more than 20 ponds and is home to a very large colony of great crested newts, together with smooth newts, palmate newts, common frogs, common toads and other wildlife.

Summerlee Heritage Park (NS 729 655) in Coatbridge is a site of great interest for wildlife and history, and has an industrial wildlife trail.

Four-spotted chaser dragonfly.

© Jackie Gilliland

Opening hours and facilities

Facilities: A visitor centre with toilets (including wheelchair-accessible ones) is open Oct–March 10.30am–4pm; April–May 10.30–5pm; June–Aug 10.30–7.30pm (tel. 01236 422 257). A network of paths provides easy access to all areas of the park and most of these are suitable for wheelchairs. There is an enclosed play area for children, a municipal golf course and pedalo boats for hire on Lochend Loch in the summer.

How to get there

By train: There are three stations within walking distance of the park.

Glasgow Queen Street to Blairhill (Drumgelloch line): from the station, turn left along Blair Rd – after about 100m the park entrance is on the right, the visitor centre 2.5km away.

Glasgow Queen Street to Gartcosh (Cumbernauld and Falkirk Grahamston lines): from the station, walk about 1.5km south along the A752 (Coatbridge Rd/Gartcosh Rd) and turn left into Townhead Rd – the visitor centre is on the right.

Glasgow Central to Bargeddie Station (Wifflet line): from the station, turn left and walk north for 1.5km along the A752 from where there are two places to enter the park.

By car: From Glasgow, take the M8 until Junction 8 and then the A89 (Coatbridge Rd) to the Bargeddie roundabout. Turn left on to the A752 (Gartcosh Rd), and after 1.5km turn right on to Townhead Rd: the visitor centre and car park are on your right. If you are coming from the east, leave the A8 at the junction for the Showcase Cinemas and follow the A752, which is signposted for Gartcosh.

Maps: Glasgow street map; OS Landranger 64, Explorer 342; a free map of the park is available at the visitor centre.

Cathkin Marsh

A beautiful area of wetland surrounded by green fields

Grid ref: Reserve entrance NS 620 570

Cathkin Marsh Wildlife Reserve is a hidden gem amongst green fields between Glasgow and East Kilbride. This beautiful area of fen and marshy grassland is home to a wide range of wildlife. The reserve belongs to the Scottish Wildlife Trust.

The reserve was once a shallow loch, which gradually filled up with vegetation over hundreds of years and formed a fen. Fens differ from bogs in that they receive their nutrients from groundwater, which is usually less acidic than rainwater. They provide important benefits, including reducing the risk of floods, improving water quality and providing habitats for distinctive plant and animal communities. Fens are relatively rare in central Scotland because many have been reclaimed for agriculture.

Cathkin Marsh is great for the botanically minded. It has a patch of developing peat bog, tall herb fen vegetation and marsh-loving flowers, such as ragged robin, northern marsh-orchid and marsh cinquefoil. Locally uncommon species found on the reserve include tea-leaved willow and slender tufted-sedge.

The reserve is also home to a number of notable breeding birds including grasshopper warbler and reed bunting, and provides a valuable wintering habitat for both common and jack snipe. In addition to the bird life, there are many mammals present here, with roe deer and red foxes seen throughout the year. The reserve teems with insect life, particularly during spring and summer when dragonflies, damselflies and butterflies are on the wing. Look out for the aptly named orange-tip and green-veined white butterflies amongst the fen vegetation, seeking out cuckoo flowers on which they lay their eggs.

Highlights

The reed bunting is a slim sparrow-sized bird with a long, deeply notched tail, white collar and drooping moustache. During the summer the male has a distinctive black head, whilst in winter both males and females have brown streaked heads. In flight the tail looks black with broad white edges. Reed buntings predominantly eat seeds, but also insects during the breeding season. More than 50 per cent of reed bunting chicks are not fathered by the pair male, but are the result of an adulterous liaison – the highest recorded rate of any bird.

© Kim McEwen

Cathkin Marsh.

© Kim McEwen

Male orange-tip butterfly.

Facilities

The reserve has 1.5km of footpath that is suitable for wheelchairs, a wheelchair-accessible bird hide and an information panel.

How to get there

By train: Glasgow Central low level to Busby (East Kilbride line). From the station walk 2km north-east along Carmunnock Rd (B759) to Carmunnock. From here continue to walk north along Cathkin Rd (B759) for about 750m, then take the first right on to a minor road: the reserve is located 1.5km on the left.

By bus: First bus 31 goes to Carmunnock: from here follow directions under 'By train'.

By car: Take the M77 from Glasgow, exit at Junction 3 and follow the A726 to East Kilbride. After 5.5km turn left on to Carmunnock Rd (B759) to Carmunnock, then follow directions under 'By train'. There is space for two cars to park opposite the entrance to the reserve.

Maps: Glasgow street map; OS Landranger 64, Explorer 342; a map of the reserve can be downloaded from www.clydeswt.org.

Activities

There are regular events led by SWT Rangers. For more details phone 0131 312 7765 or email enquiries@swt.org.uk.

Also nearby

Wester Kittochside (NS 604 556), about 2km to the south-west, a National Trust for Scotland site encompassing the National Museum of Rural Life and species-rich grassland.

Male reed bunting.

© T Norman Tait

Bothwell Castle Grounds

Broadleaved policy woodland on the estate of a thirteenth-century castle

Grid ref: Bothwell Castle NS 688 593

The grounds of Bothwell Castle extend over 73 hectares of land on either side of the River Clyde between Uddingston and Bothwell. They are important for broadleaved, mixed and yew woodland, communities of higher plants – particularly flowering plants – and beetles associated with dead wood. The grounds are designated as a Site of Special Scientific Interest. The remains of the thirteenth-century castle are currently under the management of Historic Scotland.

There is a diverse range of tree species at the site, including oak, ash and rowan, with willow and alder in wetter areas. The shrub layer consists of hazel, bird cherry, elder, holly and hawthorn. Some of the large, old trees such as yew are thought to be remnants of specimen trees planted between the late 1600s and early 1700s.

The beetle *Orchesia undulata*.

Ramsons.

© South Lanarkshire Countryside Ranger Service

The site is also noted for its flowering plant community. There is a range of helleborine orchids, including broad-leaved and Young's helleborine. There are also species such as pendulous sedge and tuberous comfrey, which have a limited distribution in Britain. Typical woodland ground flora at the site includes snowdrop, bluebell, dog's mercury, ramsons, wood-sedge, common enchanter's nightshade, wood avens, hedge woundwort, primrose and sanicle. Non-flowering plants recorded here include wood horsetail, scaly male-fern, hard shield-fern and hart's-tongue fern. Non-native invasive species are evident: rhododendron in the woodland and Japanese knotweed and Indian balsam along the edge of the river.

Look out for grey heron, mallard, goosander, mute swan, kingfisher and goldeneye, which you may see on the River

Clyde as it flows through the woodland. Birds in the woods include sparrowhawk, tawny owl, great spotted woodpecker, treecreeper, blackcap, wren and chiffchaff. Otters are present along the river, with badger, red fox, roe deer and grey squirrel in and around the wood.

Bothwell Castle.

Opening hours and facilities

Bothwell Castle, for which there is an admission charge, has toilets and a shop. It is open April–Sept Mon–Sun 9.30am–5.30pm; Oct Mon–Sun 9.30am–4.30pm; Nov–March Wed–Sat 9.30am–4.30pm. For more details phone 01698 816 894 or see www.historic-scotland.gov.uk.

How to get there

By train: Glasgow Central low level to Uddingston (Motherwell/Lanark lines). Exit on to the main road and turn right. Follow tourist signs to Bothwell castle: turn right down Belshill Rd, which becomes Castle Ave, and follow this to the turn-off on the right-hand side for Bothwell Castle. This walk is about 2km. Alternatively, from the station follow the path beside the railway tracks at the end of the car park (heading away from the main road). Cross the road to join Kyle Park Drive for about 100m, then follow the walkway behind the houses. This joins the Clyde Walkway under the rail bridge: keep on the path on this side of the river for about 2km to reach Bothwell Castle.

By bus: First bus 255: alight at Uddingston Cross after the train station and follow directions as above.

By car: Take the M74 to Junction 5: follow the A725 (W) (Bellshill Rd) towards Bellshill, then take the right turn into the B7071 for Bothwell. Follow signs for Uddingston or tourist signs for Bothwell Castle. Free parking is available.

Maps: Glasgow street map; OS Landranger 64, Explorer 342.

Highlights

Bothwell Castle Grounds are a designated SSSI because of the presence of saproxylic flies and beetles: those that are associated with dead wood or fungi that grow on dead wood. Beetles noted on site include the nationally rare *Enicmus rugosus*; a species associated with beech and oak, *Cerylon fagi*; a wood-boring weevil, *Pentarthrum huttoni*; and a weevil associated with regenerating oak, *Coeliodes ruber*. Adult forms of beetles, for example a false darkling beetle, *Orchesia undulata,* and a scarce fungus beetle, *Hallomenus binotatus*, can be seen feeding from flower-rich grasslands.

Also nearby

The Clyde Walkway passes through the wood. This 64km route stretches from the West End of Glasgow to the Falls of Clyde at New Lanark.

159

Calderglen Country Park

Gorge woodland and grassland on a historic estate near East Kilbride

Grid ref: Visitor centre NS 654 526

Calderglen Country Park was opened officially in 1982, combining the two previously separate estates of Calderwood and Torrance. It is located at the eastern edge of East Kilbride, to the south-east of Glasgow. From the centre of the park nature trails run 4km north, past the site of the now demolished Calderwood Castle, and 4km south to Langlands Moss Local Nature Reserve. The country park encompasses gorge woodland and grassland, parts of which are listed Sites of Importance for Nature Conservation. A roughly 2km stretch of the Rotten Calder river and surrounding habitat, from NS 658 547 northward, is a Site of Special Scientific Interest.

The Rotten Calder has cut into sandstone and limestone creating a steep gorge with lots of waterfalls. Part of the site is designated a SSSI for the presence of an almost continuous section through Carboniferous sedimentary rock layers – the Lawmuir Formation, the Lower Limestone Formation and the lower part of the Limestone Coal Formation (about 331 to 325 million years old). The presence

Bluebell.

of fossils including the bivalve mollusc *Posidonia becheri,* also found in the late Dinantian rocks of northern England, has allowed a rare correlation to be made between the ages of the sequences in these two areas.

The semi-natural woodlands of Calderglen are centred along the river gorge. While there are patches of conifer plantation, the gorge is primarily broadleaved woodland with beech, ash, sycamore, birch, wych elm and oak. The ground layer supports a wealth of typical woodland flora with carpets of bluebell and ramsons in spring, along with lesser celandine, dog's mercury, wood anemone, woodruff, wood sorrel, sanicle and wood and water avens. Rocky outcrops are home to a variety of ferns, mosses and liverworts.

Along the length of the river, kingfisher, dipper, grey wagtail and grey heron can be seen. Look for otter footprints under the bridge at Strathaven Road (NS 647 516). In the woods there are badger setts, red fox dens and plenty of rabbits. Daubenton's and pipistrelle bats can also be found in the park. Garden and woodland birds such as great spotted woodpecker, tawny owl, long-tailed tit and mistle thrush are present. Common blue, red admiral, painted lady,

Scarlet elf cup fungus.

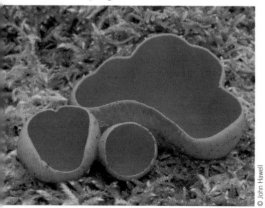

Beech trees beside the Rotten Calder.

green-veined white and orange-tip butterflies have all been noted along the Langlands trail. Sand martins have been seen along the banks of the stream here.

Highlights

Plants of interest include bird's-nest orchid, alternate-leaved golden-saxifrage, touch-me-not balsam and oak fern. Fungi are plentiful in autumn, including horn of plenty and white oyster fungus, with scarlet elf cup a feature during spring.

Activities

Regular events are held at the country park: for details phone 01355 236 644 or see www.southlanarkshire.gov.uk, where you can also download trail leaflets.

Also nearby

Langlands Moss LNR (NS 635 511) is a lowland raised bog about 4km to the south-west, which can be reached by car or on foot from Calderglen. Heather dominates the site with hare's-tail cottongrass, sphagnum mosses, cranberry, bog asphodel, cloudberry, round-leaved sundew and lesser twayblade orchid. Common lizards can be seen basking on the boardwalk supports on hot days, with

dragonflies and damselflies over the open pools of water. For more information contact the Ranger Service at Calderglen (tel. 01355 236 644) or see the website of the Friends of Langlands Moss: www.folm-ek.org.

Opening hours and facilities

The park itself is open from dawn to dusk all year. The visitor centre is open Oct–March 11am–4pm and April–Sept 10.30am–5pm. It includes a conservatory/zoo (for which there is a small charge), a café and toilets, including wheelchair-accessible ones. The Walk the Mile trail is without steps, though roughly surfaced.

How to get there

By bus: First bus 20 comes closest to the park. Alight at Strathaven Rd before the flats on the left. Then follow the main road for 10 minutes to reach Calderglen.

By car: From the M74 Junction 5 take the A725 expressway to East Kilbride, and then follow signs to Strathaven or tourist signs to Calderglen, which is on the A726 (Strathaven Rd). Free parking is available.

Maps: Glasgow street map; OS Landranger 64, Explorer 334.

161

Chatelherault Country Park

Ancient oak trees, rare beetles and Cadzow cattle

Grid ref: Visitor centre NS 736 539

Chatelherault Country Park, once the hunting grounds of the dukes of Hamilton, consists of more than 150 hectares of mixed woodlands. The Avon Water runs through the park, and on the steepest slopes there are relatively undisturbed remnants of the broadleaved woodland that would have dominated in this region for thousands of years. These ancient gorge woods are now part of the Clyde Valley Woodlands National Nature Reserve, and parts are designated as Sites of Special Scientific Interest.

The mixed woodland comprises ash, elm and oak with local sections of birch and alder. There are also areas of conifer plantation, and other non-natives such as sycamore and rhododendron. Ground flora includes bluebell, ramsons, wood anemone, lesser celandine, dog's mercury, common spotted-orchid, wood and water avens, red campion, herb-robert, broad-

The Duke's Bridge crosses the deep gorge of the Avon Water.

© John Hawell

leaved helleborine and alternate-leaved and opposite-leaved golden-saxifrage.

Fungi are plentiful, with species such as trumpet chanterelle, beech milkcap, blackening brittlegill, wood hedgehog, orange peel and beefsteak fungus. Interesting plants recorded in the park include hard shield-fern, hart's-tongue fern, great horsetail, pendulous sedge, wood fescue, meadow saxifrage, toothwort and moschatel.

There are many badger setts within Chatelherault on the steep, undisturbed woodland slopes. Other mammals include roe deer, red fox and common and soprano pipistrelle and Daubenton's bats. Signs of otters can be seen along the river bank; other river species include kingfisher, dipper, grey wagtail, Atlantic salmon and trout. Birds in the gorge woodland include jay, great spotted woodpecker, tawny owl, raven, woodcock and goldcrest.

Various hoverflies, which are associated with different types of habitat found at Chatelherault, have been recorded: *Criorhina berberina* larvae are found in dead wood and *Portevinia maculata* larvae develop in ramsons bulbs. During the summer months, adult hoverflies can be seen in sunny glades and gardens, with other insects such as small tortoiseshell, comma, peacock and ringlet butterflies and migrant silver Y moths.

White Cadzow cattle can generally be seen in the fields in front of the main buildings: this rare breed has grazed in the parkland of Chatelherault for many centuries.

Highlights
The Cadzow oak parkland dates from the mid twelfth century and one or two of the trees present today may survive from this original planting. A few of the 360 ancient trees are within the country park, the remainder are

The ancient Cadzow oaks.

visible in the adjacent Hamilton High Parks SSSI. The Barncluith path from Cadzow Castle goes along the edge of the SSSI and many of the oaks can be seen from here. The great age of the oaks gives them strange twisted shapes and a high habitat value for wildlife. The trees are important for several beetles: including the hairy fungus beetle *Mycetophagus populi,* not known at any other site in Scotland, and *Ptenidium gressneri* and *Ctesuis serra,* which are in only one other Scottish site. Other nationally scarce beetles found here are *Phyllodrepoidea crenata, Thymalus limbatus* and the weevil *Cerylon fagi.*

Activities

Regular events such as treasure trails, weekly health walks and fungi identification and bat walks are offered – for details phone 01698 426 213 or see www.southlanarkshire.gov.uk, from which you can also download trail leaflets. The woodland paths are suitable for mountain bikes.

Also nearby

South Haugh SINC (NS 732 553), an area of wetland and grassland where the Avon Water joins the Clyde (NS 737 560). This can be reached from Chatelherault via National Cycle Route 74.

Lesser celandines and wood anemone.

Opening hours and facilities

The park itself is open from dawn to dusk all year. Toilets are available at the visitor centre, including wheelchair-accessible ones, which also houses a café and gift shop, and exhibitions about natural and local history: open Mon–Sat 10am–5pm, Sun 11am–5pm. The historical rooms of the main buildings are open Mon–Thurs 10am–4.30pm (wheelchair accessible).

There are woodland trails throughout the park, ranging from 1km long to an 8km route.

How to get there

By train: Glasgow Central Station low level to Chatelherault (Larkhall line), ten minutes' walk from the park.

By bus: From Hamilton Bus Station, McKindless 31, Whitelaw 250, 253, 254 and 255, and Stuart's 317: there are bus stops at the entrance to Chatelherault.

By car: Chatelherault is on the A72 (Carlisle Rd) at Ferniegair, between Hamilton and Larkhall. Exit the M74 at Hamilton (Junction 6) and follow tourist signs for Chatelherault. Car parking is free.

Maps: Glasgow street map; OS Landranger 64, Explorer 343.

Baron's Haugh RSPB Reserve

A year-round wildlife spectacle close to the heart of Motherwell

Grid ref: Car park NS 755 553

Baron's Haugh is a wonderfully diverse reserve with a range of habitats, including freshwater pools and ancient woodland. It is close to the centre of Motherwell but still in a rural area by the Clyde – 'haugh' means a low-lying meadow beside a river. The 100-hectare site originally formed part of the historic Dalzell Estate, home to the Hamilton family, who lived in the nearby Dalzell House from 1647 until the 1980s. Baron's Haugh was purchased by RSPB Scotland in 1983 and is now managed as a wildlife reserve.

A sluice linked to the Clyde enables the control of water levels in the wetlands to benefit waders in the spring and autumn and wildfowl in the winter. Cattle help to provide areas of short grass and churned-up ground to encourage breeding waders. Where safe, the trees on the reserve are allowed to mature and decay to provide a rich habitat for fungi, insects and the many different animals that feed on them.

More than 140 different species of bird have been recorded at the reserve. In spring and summer there is an influx of breeding warblers including grasshopper warbler, willow warbler and blackcap. Tufted duck, gadwall and little grebe all breed here, and it is also good for water rail.

In the autumn, the site attracts passage waders – migrating birds stopping for a short time. There are large numbers of lapwing as well as more unusual species such as black-tailed godwit, green sandpiper and ruff. Water levels are raised in the winter months, bringing in birds such as wigeon, teal and whooper swan, and affording good views of hunting raptors such as peregrine.

Badgers are seen on the reserve fairly regularly and roe deer and red foxes are

Looking north across Baron's Haugh.

© Andy Hay (rspb-images.com)

Lapwing.

© Sue Tranter (rspb-images.com)

common. Otters use the area and lucky visitors may get views of them from the hides.

To date, 17 species of butterfly have been recorded, including the locally abundant orange-tip and rarer comma.

Highlights

Baron's Haugh is one of the best sites in the area for breeding gadwall, with around six pairs. Nuthatches breed in the woodlands and are close to their northernmost range. In the summer, the reserve provides excellent views of sand martin colonies in the banks of the River Clyde – the birds are attracted by newly exposed sand banks created by the river, which meanders at this point and changes its banks from year to year. The autumn and winter months are notable for their large numbers of waders and wildfowl.

Activities

Guided walks take place about once a month. These can include evening badger and bat walks. RSPB Scotland is keen to recruit volunteers to help work on a

multitude of tasks around the reserve – for more details phone 0141 331 0993 or email BaronsHaugh@rspb.org.uk.

Also nearby

Dalzell Estate is adjacent, with a designed landscape of tree-lined avenues and planted woodlands. Within the grounds is the ancient Covenanter's Oak, which is of historical interest. For more information see www.dalzellandbaronshaugh.co.uk.

Facilities

There are four basic hides around the site with signposted trails around them. Most paths are suitable for wheelchairs, with the exception of the circular trail.

The site has a 'mobitour' – an audio guide operated through visitors' own mobile phones by dialling numbers on the information boards and marked posts.

How to get there

By train: Glasgow Central low level to Airbles (Motherwell line). From the station, turn right on to Airbles Rd. Turn right at the second mini-roundabout on to Adele St, and at the end of the road turn left and then right on to Manse Rd to reach the reserve entrance.

By bus: First bus 245 (Forgewood–North Lodge Circular) goes past Motherwell train station at Brandon Parade and runs to North Lodge Ave and Adele St – from where follow the directions given in the 'By train' details above.

By car: From Junction 6 of the M74, take the A723 road to Motherwell. Bear right at the next traffic lights, signposted to Wishaw. Turn right at the third mini-roundabout (Adele St), and follow the road to the end: turn left, then immediately right to enter the reserve – the car park is on the right.

Maps: Glasgow street map; OS Landranger 64, Explorer 343.

Falls of Clyde

Spectacular waterfalls within the New Lanark World Heritage Site

Grid refs: Car park NS 882 425; visitor centre NS 881 424; Corra Linn NS 882 413

The Falls of Clyde have been attracting visitors for hundreds of years; the tallest waterfall, Corra Linn, is nearly 30m high. Along the sides of the river, ancient woodland on steep rocky cliffs supports a diverse range of plants and insects: on account of this, the site is designated as part of the Clyde Valley Woodlands National Nature Reserve. Part of the Falls of Clyde is a Site of Special Scientific Interest and a Special Area of Conservation. The reserve, which is managed by the Scottish Wildlife Trust, is within the New Lanark World Heritage Site, an 18th-century mill complex.

The deep gorge was cut at the end of the last Ice Age, after glacial deposits had blocked the original channel of the Clyde. It reveals the joints, faults and layers of Devonian or Old Red Sandstone rocks – greywackes, sandstones and shales. The wider surrounding countryside is covered in the rolling landscape of glacial drift sands and gravels.

The reserve has a rich botanical interest. Oak and birch dominate the higher and drier ground, while ash and alder favour the springs, seepages and river edges. Ground flora includes bluebell, ramsons and sanicle, with some rarer species such as meadow saxifrage, moschatel and, in the gorge, purple saxifrage. Some impressive old oak, beech and conifer trees remain on both sides of the river, surviving from earlier designed landscapes. Parts of the wider reserve are slowly being restored from conifer plantations, dating from the 1950s, to broadleaved woodland. An area of neutral grassland is managed as a wildflower meadow.

The diverse habitats support an equally diverse fauna. The most obvious include the woodland birds such as great spotted woodpecker, jay and woodcock. Badger, bats, roe deer, red fox and tawny owl are often spotted in the evenings, and otter, goosander, dipper and grey wagtail are regularly seen at places along the river. Common frog and common darter dragonfly use the dipping pond. Chimney sweeper moths and orange-tip, ringlet and small tortoiseshell butterflies are often spotted, and the comma butterfly has been recorded since 2008. The ancient woodland is also important for dead-wood invertebrates, including long horn beetles, wood wasps and ichneumon flies.

© Richard Sutcliffe

Corra Linn in spate.

© David Palmer (www.photoscot.co.uk)

© Bryan Bowes

Above: Badger.

Left: Peregrine falcon.

Highlights

The key species that can be seen at the site include peregrine falcons, which have bred on the reserve since 1997. They can be observed from a special hide from April to June. Badgers can often be seen on organized badger watches. The scenery on the walk through the reserve past Corra Linn and Bonnington Linn, the furthest upstream of the falls, is spectacular and you may glimpse otters, dippers and occasionally kingfishers.

Activities

The SWT Reserve Rangers run a variety of activities, including guided walks and Operation Peregrine. For further information phone 01555 665 262 or see www.swt.org.uk.

Also nearby

Lower Nethan Gorge (NS 820 466), a SWT reserve just off the A72 about 7km north-west of Lanark is part of the Clyde Valley Woodlands NNR. It has ash and elm woodland, which supports a variety of birds and insects.

Facilities

There is a visitor centre with toilets and a gift shop, which is open March–Dec daily 11am–5pm, Jan–Feb daily 12pm–4pm. It also has an exhibition area, for which there is a small entrance charge. A café and toilets are also available in New Lanark's Mill 3.

How to get there

By train: Glasgow Central low level to Lanark. From the bus stance next to the station, take Stuart's Coaches 135, or you could walk in about 25 minutes: exit the station on to Bannatyne St and turn right – at the traffic lights, turn left down the South Vennel and left again at the bottom of the road on to the Wellgate. Cross over to Braxfield Rd and follow this to the New Lanark World Heritage Site.

By bus: Irvine's bus 240/240X to Lanark bus stance. Then take Stuart's 135 from beside the train station to New Lanark – a 5-minute journey – or follow the directions in the 'By train' details.

By car: Exit the M74 at Junction 7 and take the A72 to Lanark. Turn right on to the A73 and follow the brown tourist signs for New Lanark to the World Heritage Site car park.

Maps: Glasgow street map; OS Landranger 72, Explorer 335; a reserve map can be downloaded from www.swt.org.uk.

How to find out more

If you would like to find out more about the sites mentioned in this book, or about wildlife and conservation in the area in general, the following contacts may be useful. All details were correct at the time of printing.

Local authority websites

East Dunbartonshire
www.eastdunbarton.gov.uk – search for Local Biodiversity Action Plan.

East Renfrewshire
www.eastrenfrewshire.gov.uk – go to Planning and the Environment, then Natural Environment, then Biodiversity (where you can download LBAP documents), Nature Conservation (for information on SSSIs) and Greenspaces.

Glasgow City Council
www.glasgow.gov.uk – follow links for Residents, then Parks and Outdoors, then Countryside Rangers, from where you can download the Countryside Events Programme and read a Ranger's Diary. You can also follow links to Ecology to find information about the LBAP, wildlife sites and conservation action, read a wildlife diary and download copies of the Glasgow Biodiversity News. The link to Parks and Gardens takes you to more information about some of the 90 parks and formal gardens in the city, and following the link for Visitors and selecting What's On takes you to the listing Events in the Park this Week.

Inverclyde
www.inverclyde.gov.uk – go to Planning and the Environment, then Conservation, then Nature Conservation and Biodiversity. Here you can access information about the LBAP and download maps of all SSSIs and SINCs within Inverclyde.

North Lanarkshire
www.northlanarkshire.gov.uk – go to Tourism and Visitor Attractions, then Countryside, Wildlife, Parks, Gardens and Open Spaces. Here there is information about a variety of open spaces, the countryside and leisure, countryside management and conservation.

Renfrewshire
www.renfrewshire.gov.uk – go to Leisure and Culture, then Parks and Recreation and Parks and Gardens.

South Lanarkshire
www.southlanarkshire.gov.uk – go to Parks and Countryside, then Country Parks and Rangers. If you select Related Forms, Publications, you can download leaflets for trails at Calderglen and Chatelherault country parks and along the Clyde Walkway.

West Dunbartonshire
www.west-dunbarton.gov.uk – go to Environment and then Biodiversity to find information about the Dunbartonshire LBAP.

Contacts for Countryside Ranger Services

Clyde Muirshiel Regional Park: tel. 01505 614 791, www.clydemuirshiel.co.uk.
Dams to Darnley Country Park: tel. 0141 577 4053/4, www.damstodarnley.org.
East Dunbartonshire and Mugdock Country Park: tel. 0141 956 6586, www.mugdock-country-park.org.uk.
Glasgow City Council: tel. 0141 276 0924, www.glasgow.gov.uk.
North Lanarkshire: tel. nos 01236 422 257 (Drumpellier Country Park) and 01236 780 636 (Palacerigg Country Park), www.northlanarkshire.gov.uk.
South Lanarkshire: tel. nos 01698 426 213 (Chatelherault Country Park) and 01355 236 644 (Calderglen Country Park), www.southlanarkshire.gov.uk.
Renfrewshire: tel. 0141 884 3794 (Land Services Officers), www.renfrewshire.gov.uk.
West Dunbartonshire: tel. 01389 737 000, www.wdcweb.info.

Local Biodiversity Action Plans and Biodiversity Officers

To find out more about LBAPs and for contact details for all the local Biodiversity Officers in the area visit the Biodiversity Scotland website www.biodiversityscotland. gov.uk (to be relaunched early 2011), phone 01463 725 325 or email bit@snh.gov.uk.

Natural history societies and similar organizations

There are many interest groups in the Glasgow area which arrange talks, excursions and so on. Those listed below are particularly active.

Butterfly Conservation
Also interested in moths, the Glasgow and south-west Scotland branch runs indoor meetings in winter and excursions in summer – see www.southwestscotland-butterflies.org.uk.

Clyde Amphibian and Reptile Group
CARG volunteers promote the conservation of amphibians and reptiles in the Clyde area – see www.carg.webnode.com.

Clyde Bat Group
Concerned with bat conservation, members undertake surveying and run guided walks and talks – see www.clydebatgroup.org.

Friends of the River Kelvin (FORK)
This group aims to protect, conserve and preserve the River Kelvin, its tributaries and immediate environs – see www.fork.org.uk.

Glasgow Natural History Society
GNHS encourages the study of natural history and holds evening meetings, outdoor excursions and occasional conferences. Members receive *The Glasgow Naturalist* and have access to the society's library – see www.glasgownaturalhistory.org.uk.

Geological Society of Glasgow
The society holds lectures and organizes outdoor excursions. Members receive the *Scottish Journal of Geology* and have access to the society's library and the main library of the University of Glasgow. The subgroup Strathclyde RIGS are involved in conserving geological sites. Leaflets about Ardmore Point, Campsie Glen, Fossil Grove and Balmaha can be downloaded from the society's website www.geologyglasgow.org.uk or obtained by emailing strathrigs@tiscali.co.uk.

Hamilton Natural History Society
The society runs evening meetings and excursions – for details contact the secretary by phoning 01355 225 500 or emailing ensignro@tiscali.co.uk.

Paisley Natural History Society
Evening meetings and excursions, mainly in Renfrewshire – see www.paisleynaturalhistorysociety.org.uk.

RSPB
The Glasgow group holds evening meetings and runs field trips – phone 0141 331 0993 or see www.rspb.org.uk/scotland.

Scottish Ornithologists' Club
The Clyde branch holds evening meetings in Glasgow and arranges excursions – for details contact the secretary, Hayley Douglas, on 07715 634 079 or see www.the-soc.org.uk.

Scottish Wildlife Trust
The SWT works to protect Scotland's natural environment and wildlife and runs many events. To find out more phone 0131 312 7765 or see www.clydeswt.org, where there is information about reserves (including reserve maps etc to download), activities and how to get involved. See also www.swt.org.uk.

Other organizations

British Waterways Scotland
Phone 0141 332 6936 or visit www. scottishcanals.co.uk. Information leaflets etc are available in person from Canal House, Applecross Street, Glasgow G4 9SP.

Clyde River Foundation
This charity researches the ecology of the Clyde and its tributaries and promotes environmental education and sustainable management – to find out more phone 0141 330 5080 or visit www. clyderiverfoundation.org.

Glasgow and Clyde Valley Green Network Partnership
An ambitious 20-year programme which will link parks, walkways, woodlands and countryside along miles of paths and cycle routes – see www.gcvgreennetwork.gov.uk.

Loch Lomond and the Trossachs National Park
Tel. 01389 722 600, www.lochlomond-trossachs.org.

National Trust for Scotland
The NTS has more than 100 places to visit, including historic sites and outstanding countryside. Tel. 0844 493 2100, www.nts.org.uk.

Scottish Natural Heritage
The telephone number of SNH at Clydebank is 0141 951 4488, the website www.snh.org.uk. SNH have just produced a booklet called 'Simple pleasures, easily found: Get out and about in Glasgow', which lists many greenspaces in and around Glasgow.

Scotland's National Nature Reserves
NNRs help protect wildlife and landscapes – see www.nnr-scotland.org.uk and select individual reserves for more information.

The Scottish Outdoor Access Code
Visit www.outdooraccess-scotland.com to find all you need to know about statutory access rights and responsibilities.

Glasgow Health Walks
Free short walks led by trained volunteers – for more information see www.glasgowlife. org.uk/healthwalks or phone the Walk Glasgow Co-ordinator on 0141 287 0963.

Publications about the local area

Wild Plants of Glasgow, by JH Dickson, Aberdeen University Press, 1991 (ISBN 0 08 041200 9).

The Changing Flora of Glasgow: Urban and Rural Through the Centuries, by JH Dickson, P Macpherson and K Watson, Edinburgh University Press, 2001 (ISBN 0 7486 1397 8).

The Flora of Renfrewshire, by Keith Watson, is being prepared and it is hoped it will be published in the near future.

Geological Excursions around Glasgow and Girvan, by JD Lawson and DS Weedon, Geological Society of Glasgow, 1992 (ISBN 0 902892 09 6).

Landscape fashioned by geology – Glasgow and Ayrshire, Scottish Natural Heritage, 2006 (ISBN 185397451X).

The Butterflies of South West Scotland – An atlas of their distribution, by K Futter, R Sutcliffe and others, Argyll Publishing, 2006 (ISBN 1 902831 95 0).

An Annotated Checklist of the Larger Moths of Stirlingshire, West Perthshire and Dunbartonshire, by John Knowler, Glasgow Natural History Society, 2010 (ISBN 978-0956529503).

Archaeology Around Glasgow: 50 remarkable sites to visit, by Susan Hothersall, Culture and Sport Glasgow (Glasgow Museums), 2007, revised 2010 (ISBN 978 0 90752 91 7), which highlights fascinating archaeological sites to visit over an area very similar to that covered by this publication.

Museums to visit

Natural history specimens are on display, or may be available for examination by appointment, at several museums in the area. There is free entry to those listed below.

Kelvingrove Art Gallery and Museum has extensive natural history displays, including ones about Scottish and local wildlife, the birds most likely to be seen in gardens, endangered and extinct species and fossils. (Open Monday–Thursday and Saturday 10am–5pm, Friday and Sunday 11am–5pm; Argyle Street, Glasgow G3 8AG; tel. 0141 276 9599; www.glasgowmuseums.com.)

Glasgow Museums Resource Centre (GMRC) is a publicly accessible museum storage facility and visitor centre, which houses the majority of Glasgow Museums' 585,000 natural history objects (you can read about these at www.glasgowmuseums.com – select Collections and then Collections Navigator). Tours of the natural history store can be arranged. (Open Tuesday–Thursday and Saturday 10am–5pm, Friday and Sunday 11am–5pm, but please book visits in advance; 200 Woodhead Road, Nitshill, Glasgow G53 7NN; tel. 0141 276 9300; www.glasgowmuseums.com.)

The Hunterian Museum houses the University of Glasgow's geological displays and some zoology exhibits, including Scottish dinosaur remains; the Zoology Museum, in the nearby Graham Kerr Building, has most of the university's zoology collections. (Both sites open Monday–Friday 9.30am–5pm; University of Glasgow, University Avenue, Glasgow G12 8QQ; tel. nos 0141 330 4221 and 0141 330 4772; www.hunterian.gla.ac.uk.)

Paisley Museum and Art Galleries has a natural history collection which is mostly from the Renfrewshire area. Paisley Museum also maintains a biological records centre which collates and records information about species and habitats within the local area. (Open Tuesday–Saturday 10am–5pm, Sunday 2–5pm; High Street, Paisley PA1 2BD; tel. 0141 889 3151; www.renfrewshire.gov.uk.)

McLean Museum and Art Gallery contains a diverse range of natural history material including minerals, rocks, fossils, plants and animals from all over the world. The key display is of African mammals, birds and fish from the RL Scott collection. (Open Monday–Saturday 10am–5pm, except public holidays; 15 Kelly Street, Greenock, Inverclyde PA16 8JX; tel. 01475 715 624; www.inverclyde.gov.uk.)

Glasgow Museums Biological Records Centre GMBRC holds biological and environmental information mainly from Glasgow, East Dunbartonshire, West Dunbartonshire, Renfrewshire, East Renfrewshire and Inverclyde. This data is made available for environmental decision-making, education, research and other uses for public benefit. More records for the area are always welcome. If you like to pass on your own records of species that you have seen, or obtain further information, please email biological.records@glasgowlife.org.uk or phone 0141 276 9330.

Index to common names of minerals, fossils, plants, fungi and animals mentioned in the text, with scientific names where individual species are listed. References to illustrations are in italic type.